Evangelical Style
AND
Lutheran Substance

Facing America's Mission Challenge

by

David S. Luecke

Publishing House
St. Louis

Contents

Unless otherwise noted, the Scripture quotations in this publication are from The Holy Bible: NEW INTERNATIONAL VERSION, © 1973, 1978, 1984 by the International Bible Society. Used by permission of Zondervan Bible Publishers.

Biblical references marked RSV are from the Revised Standard Version of the Bible, copyrighted 1946, 1952, ©1971, 1973. Used by permission.

Quotations marked KJV are from the King James or Authorized Version of the Bible.

Copyright © 1988 by Concordia Publishing House
3558 S. Jefferson Avenue, St. Louis, MO 63118-3968
Manufactured in the United States of America

Library of Congress Cataloging in Publication Data.

Luecke, David S., 1940–
    Evangelical style and mainline substance: evangelical insights for Lutheran evangelism/ by David S. Luecke.
      p.   cm.
    ISBN 0-570-04496-0: $7.95
    1. Evangelistic work. 2. Evangelicalism. 3. Lutheran Church–Doctrines.   I. Title.
BV3793.L82   1988   88-10952
269'.2—dc19   CIP

   3   4   5   6   7   8   9   10   97   96   95   94   93   92   91   90

Acknowledgments

A writing project like this presumes much more than solitary hours in a study with books. It is the product of interaction with many different church people in different church settings. Special ones must be acknowledged.

This whole writing enterprise of looking at Evangelicals from a Lutheran viewpoint began with an invitation from Roger Leenerts, associate executive secretary of North American ministries of the Board for Mission Services of The Lutheran Church—Missouri Synod. He asked me to share a little about what I was learning at Fuller Theological Seminary as part of a church administration presentation to the North American Mission Executives Conference meeting in Phoenix in March 1985. From Valparaiso University I came to Fuller in June 1983 as vice president of seminary services and a member of the faculty of the School of Theology.

That paper led to an invitation from Robert Holst to talk to students at Christ College Irvine in February 1986 about why they should stay in Lutheranism. The distinction between village and camp church emerged out of that effort to explain why we Lutherans are the way we are in relation to Evangelicals.

The idea and outline for a book emerged in preparation for a two-day presentation for the Annual Conference of District Evangelism Executives and Chairpersons of The Lutheran Church—Missouri Synod, meeting in Pasadena in May 1986. The invitation and then readiness to have about 50 Lutheran leaders visit growing Southern California Evangelical churches came from W. Leroy Biesenthal, associate secretary of the Synod's Board of Evangelism Services. Special encouragement to get the book published came from Erwin Kolb, executive secretary of the same Board for Evangelism Services and from Edward Westcott, executive secretary of Synod's Board for Mission Services.

The material for the last chapter was developed for a presentation on the ministry and the universal priesthood for the Pastoral

3

Conference of the Southern California District of The Lutheran Church—Missouri Synod in October 1986. I am especially indebted to District President Arnold Kuntz and then President Loren Kramer for their steady and enthusiastic support.

To these should be added scores of other Lutheran leaders and church people who have given me affirmation and encouragement in this endeavor.

There would be nothing to write about without the insights and encouragement of my Evangelical colleagues at Fuller Theological Seminary. I am particularly indebted to President David Hubbard, who reached beyond their normal circles to pull in a Lutheran and who gave me continued guidance in understanding the broader environment where I landed. He also taught me much about an Evangelical style of writing that places a premium on getting the reader interested and that permits personal examples.

Carl George, director of the Charles E. Fuller Institute of Evangelism and Church Growth, was my first real contact with an Evangelical leader, and he is a fine teacher. Peter Wagner, professor of church growth in the School of World Mission, has been a constant presence and intellectual challenge. My administrative colleague Mel Robeck has been an excellent scholarly guide to an understanding of mature Pentecostalism and its history.

To these should be added scores of other Evangelical leaders, seminarians, and church people who have modeled and explained the Evangelical style.

My family—wife Marcia and children Angela, Matthew, and Sarah—merit very special public acknowledgment. They bore with me during the intense year of distraction that culminated in the manuscript. They tendered loving care and support during the period of exhaustion and recovery that followed its completion.

Thank God for the people of His church—in all their diversity.

David S. Luecke

Pasadena, Calif.

Feb. 29, 1988

PART 1

Old Churches and New Styles

Introduction

Andrew, Simon Peter's brother, was one of the two who heard what John had said and who had followed Jesus. The first thing Andrew did was to find his brother Simon and tell him, "We have found the Messiah" (that is, the Christ). And he brought him to Jesus. . . .

The next day Jesus decided to leave for Galilee. Finding Philip, he said to him, "Follow me."

. . . Philip found Nathanael and told him, "We have found the one Moses wrote about in the Law, and about whom the prophets also wrote—Jesus of Nazareth, the son of Joseph."

"Nazareth! Can anything good come from there?" Nathanael asked.

"Come and see," said Philip.

. . . Then Nathanael declared, "Rabbi, you are the Son of God; you are the King of Israel" (John 1:40–49).

This text from the Gospel According to John introduces evangelism at its exciting best. One person encounters Jesus and recognizes Him as the Savior. He immediately shares the Good News with another, who then accepts the invitation to check out the discovery. He, too, sees Jesus as Son of God and comes to faith. The circle widens.

The sequence happened twice in this account. First Andrew spent the day with Jesus. The next thing he did was to find his brother Simon Peter and tell him. Peter came and believed. The next day Jesus called Philip to follow Him. Philip found his friend Nathanael and told him to come and see. Nathanael was more cautious. But after he personally experienced Jesus' presence, Nathanael, too, believed.

That sequence has happened millions of times since. The first call to follow has been shared and repeated through the centuries until the circle has widened into the entire world.

Christians today are still dedicated to sharing the Good News of that life-changing discovery. But the results are not always the same as they were among the first followers. Neither are they always the same for one group of witnesses as they are for another. In some churches the sequence still seems to happen frequently. They grow. Other churches try. Yet their invitations are not accepted, and their gathering of followers declines.

Stories of growing Christian churches are prevalent. Many can be found in America and even more in Asia, Africa, and South America. Most Christians in this country can find nearby examples of local congregations that are steadily or even dramatically widening their circle of fellowship. These churches seem to have an infectious spirit. What they share is contagious. The members are excited. They invite others to experience what they believe and do. The others accept the invitation, and they, too, get caught up in this church life of following Christ. Such churches have an *esprit* about them that seems to make evangelism easy.

Not all Christian churches are like that, of course. Most churches find evangelism to be more complicated. Their members want to share the Gospel, but they struggle to find the right way. What is important to them does not come across so exciting to others. Despite their efforts, few others accept the invitation to come and see. Those who do come frequently do not stay. Such churches feel the frustration of doing evangelism that brings little or no growth.

This book is about that difference. In recent years considerable scholarly effort has gone into trying to understand why some churches grow and others decline. This is not an attempt to summarize all the possible findings. It rather focuses on a fairly simple observation that can be seen in the data for the membership trends of American Protestant denominations.

Dean M. Kelly most forcefully fixed the attention of American religious leaders on that data with the 1972 publication of his book *Why Conservative Churches Are Growing.* The title conveys his primary explanation. The denominations recognized as more conservative in theology and standards of Christian living were growing. The more liberal ones were declining.[1]

There is another interpretation of the pattern apparent in the data. It does not contradict Kelly. In addition to being conservative, the denominations with the fastest rates of growth in America in recent decades are distinct products of American history, like the

8

Southern Baptists. Most celebrate beginnings of less than a hundred years ago or so, like the Assemblies of God, Seventh-Day Adventists, Jehovah's Witnesses.

The declining denominations are older. Their history is measured in hundreds of years, and most retain allegiance to their European origins. Examples are Episcopalians, Presbyterians, Methodists, United Church of Christ, and Lutherans. These well-established church bodies are frequently called "mainline," although increasingly the term "old line" is appearing in current discussions.

Old churches in particular are finding that evangelism has become complicated. What is reflected in denominational totals is experienced by thousands of local congregations that have become old in the most visible sense. With decline, they have a preponderance of older members, people in their 50s, 60s, and 70s. In American religious life today, congregations with aging membership are likely to be old also in the sense of having long memories of traditions, customs, and polity carried forward from former eras. Old churches, both in membership and in historic identity, are having particular difficulty rekindling the evangelistic spirit that gave them their earlier growth.

Leaders of old churches share many ideas for what to do about their changed circumstances of recent decades. These range all the way from doing nothing in hopes that times will change, to launching aggressive publicity campaigns to improve their public image, meanwhile trying to manage shrinking budgets. Certainly fundamental is the need to reexamine theological basics and to renew commitment to the Gospel mission that is the reason for the existence of Christian churches.

Without that commitment this book serves no purpose. Assuming their evangelical intent, it puts forward a simple, very practical suggestion to old Christian churches, of any background. Whatever else they are trying to do, they would be prudent to see what can be learned from the newer growing churches. God is at work in these newer expressions of life in Christ. What is it in their ministry and church life that He is now using so effectively to extend His kingdom among people in today's culture? Can older churches adapt newer ways of sharing the Gospel?

"Style" will be a key word in this discussion. It is used to identify the dimensions of a church's life and ministry that can be changed.

As presented in Chapter 2, the contrast is "substance," understood as the ingredients of a church's identity that are not open to change. Old churches have styles usually inherited from earlier periods of growth that were infectious for those times. Few historic churches are willing completely to abandon their distinctive style. The challenge posed here is for them to look at the styles of growing churches and to consider whether and how they might graft some of those emphases onto their own church life and outreach.

Substance remains basic, of course. To identify the specifics, however, is not the point of this effort. To explore what would generally be considered style is the concern. Some common labels, though, are appropriate for clarifying substance reference points. The theological position and agenda is conservative Evangelical Protestant. The old church perspective is particularly that of a conservative Lutheran. Not all growing churches will be of interest. The focus is on those that fit under the umbrella of Evangelicalism, as that label is now popularly used. Mormonism, for instance, is viewed as having a substance so different that it is not included. A more careful definition of Evangelicalism will be given in Chapter 4.

The substance core assumed as a common denominator in this discussion of differing styles is this conviction: God calls all people of the world to be His own. He makes that possible through His grace as He offers eternal salvation to those who personally trust in the saving work of His Son, Jesus Christ. New life in Christ brings the desire to spread the authoritative Word through which the Holy Spirit brings people to faith and sustains them in this new life. Evangelism, or the sharing of this Good News, is fundamental to what believers gathered as church should do.

That old, mainline churches with outstanding histories of Gospel ministry might have something to learn from the newer Evangelical churches is a thought which will take getting used to for some. One reaction may be not unlike that of Nathanael when Philip invited him to "Come and see." He exclaimed, "Nazareth! Can anything good come from there?" Such an insignificant place seemed an unpromising source. The Evangelical churches of today have typically come from unpromising social origins, or at least beginnings in a cultural context different from that where older churches are accustomed to ministering. But the Lord has a way of surprising us!

A word about myself. My vantage point for watching change

happen in God's church is a juxtapositioning of old church and new. I start from the perspective of an old church. Mine is The Lutheran Church—Missouri Synod. I know best Jesus' presence as it is conveyed in the Lutheran church community that nourished me as a child, trained me as a minister, and spiritually sustains me now. I hope to remain a Lutheran minister all my life.

But the Lord has also given me an unusual opportunity to go and look at Him at work in the evangelistic styles of the newer churches that have collectively come to be known as Evangelical. In recent years I have been administering and teaching at a major center of Evangelicalism, Fuller Theological Seminary. I arrived there as an experienced administrator but a novice Evangelical in 1983. In effect, the Lord called me to "Come and see." It is with insights from Christian colleagues in Evangelical churches that I talk about new styles of evangelism for old churches, particularly Lutheran churches.

While sharing my observations, I have discovered a keen interest among many pastors and church members whose roots are not in the contemporary Evangelical churches but whose evangelical desire is to see their churches grow. That is an interest heightened all the more by an increasing awareness that their customary ministry practices are not being blessed with the sort of visible growth they observe in Evangelical churches around them.

Exploring the implications of all this is the intent of the chapters ahead. Part 1 is preparation for that exploration. It offers some distinctions that can be helpful to old churches addressing questions of how to regain an infectious evangelistic spirit. Chapter 1 speaks of a future-oriented outlook. Chapter 2 suggests a mobile, tabernacle style. Chapter 3 lets us see how vision is necessary for church growth.

Part 2 discusses the principle of borrowing styles from other churches, proposes some criteria for what to look for, and offers an assessment of different Evangelical styles while suggesting some touchpoints for Lutheran adaptations.

Part 3 presents practical learnings from Evangelical styles of communicating and organizing, applied specifically to Lutherans.

May the Lord grant the blessing of new styles that fit old churches.

CHAPTER 1

Questions for Old Churches

The theme for what follows could be stated as "Come and See." That is what Philip challenged Nathanael to do. Actually Philip's phrase was a repeat of the Lord's own words. Several verses earlier in John's gospel, Jesus had this exchange with Andrew and another, who would become His first disciples.

> John . . . looked at Jesus as He walked, and said, "Behold, the Lamb of God!" The two disciples heard him say this, and they followed Jesus. Jesus turned, and saw them following, and said to them, *"What do you seek?"* And they said to Him, "Rabbi" (which means Teacher), *"where are You staying?"* And He said to them, *"Come and see."* (John 1:35–39 RSV)

Significant in this account is that Jesus began His ministry with a question. He addressed it to people who wanted to recognize Him as the Lamb of God. "What do you seek?" Jesus said to them.

Our Lord continues to ask that question of men and women of today who recognize Jesus as Lord and are following Him on a particular path of discipleship. Jesus phrased His question in the plural, to two followers. Christians today need to hear it in the plural, especially as it is addressed to followers joined together as congregations and church bodies.

The disciples' response was striking. They did not state a need or a goal. They countered with another question. "Where are You staying?" they said to Him.

What they really wanted was to discover more about Jesus. They hoped to do so by finding where He was staying. Identifying the physical location was undoubtedly less important than assessing how and with whom He was willing to spend His time. Did He make

12

any difference in the lives He touched? What could they learn from the Lamb of God about how the visible presence of God expresses itself in daily life around them?

Both questions—from Jesus and from the disciples—looked toward the future. Can churches today respond the same way the first disciples did? Old churches in particular are usually more comfortable answering questions about what they seek by talking of where they have been in the past. Specific answers about where they are going from here are more difficult to find. Christians with old church perspectives are tempted to avoid the questions of what they seek, or to settle for generalities. But those first followers can give us courage to pause and ask in response the basic, practical questions: "Where will You be, Lord," and "With whom will You want us to stay?" Then we will know what we are seeking.

"Come and see," He said to them.

Still those followers were given no answers—just a challenge to look farther. Our Lord today so often counters our questions with the encouragement to follow and keep our eyes open. We may think we know where we are going. But God has a way of surprising us. If we are able to recognize only what we have seen in the past, we will miss out on some of the new life He is ready to give us. To come and see is to be ready to explore what lies ahead.

John's gospel account never does tell us exactly where Jesus was staying that day. It was probably with people in some obscure place on the less-traveled side of the Jordan (see vv. 28, 43). But getting to one place was not the point. In His ministry Jesus was always on the move. He remains a constant frustration today for followers who want to pin Him down to a place and time they are comfortable with. Just when churches feel they have their ministry and programs figured out, Jesus has a way of calling from somewhere else: "Come and see. Look at whom I am with now. Behold what I am doing."

OLD CHURCH DIFFICULTIES

How to regain an infectious evangelistic spirit is the central question of this discussion. It is posed from the perspective of old churches that had such a spirit in former times but now struggle with no growth or even decline. "Old" is meant especially to characterize churches that carry with them memories of a long history of how their community responded to God's call in the past, sometimes going back centuries.

As stated in the Introduction, for some churches today evangelism seems relatively easy. They experience the sort of response that Andrew and Philip had in the sequences related right after these verses in John. Their invitations to others to come to Christ brought new disciples. We will be looking at such churches that seem to have an infectious spirit today, particularly as evidenced in newer, Evangelical churches.

But rather than concentrating directly on techniques of evangelism, old churches would do well first to prepare for evangelism by focusing on what was happening in the very first encounter of disciples with Jesus, before they went out to share the Good News. To be appreciated is how Andrew and another would-be disciple were feeling uneasy and open to change. Their faces must have shown that they were looking for something: Jesus read in them an invitation to ask what they were seeking. These were already disciples of John the Baptist, and they believed what God had revealed of Himself thus far. It must have been apparent that they thought there would be more.

The basic difficulty of old churches is their tendency to lose their anticipation of more to come, to think they have already discovered everything that is important. Certainly Christians who believe that Christ came, died, and rose for their salvation have seen that which is most important. Their own unique history of God's action among them also remains important. Church life is incomplete, however, if it only looks backwards. The past is a prolog of assurance that God will continue to give new life in the future. The Good News is that He is ready to make things new now, in decisive and unexpected ways, among those who first come to faith as well as with old believers. Remaining excited about discovering such God-given new life, wherever it occurs, is the key to effective evangelism.

Believers can stay on the path of discovery by accepting Jesus' challenge to "Come and see" how and with whom He is staying among people today. His initial question, "What do you seek?" is a reminder to stay on that path. In asking it of those who would follow Him, Jesus assumes their readiness to anticipate more. Certainly He asks it of those who are just finding Him. He asks it of old churches, too.

DISCOVERY THROUGH PLANNING

Particularly striking about Jesus' opening words is that He was asking a planning question. "What do you seek?" is an inquiry about purposes and goals. That question is central to planning, which is an exploratory process organizations as well as individuals use for thinking seriously about the future. It concentrates energy on clarifying purposes and discovering alternatives for accomplishing them. Leaders are especially inclined to highlight the process when their organizations face a complicated situation.

In recent decades, planning vocabulary and processes have entered into the life of many churches. I am an advocate and teacher of church planning. Churches should routinely engage themselves in the work of probing what they are trying to accomplish with God's past blessings and how they can be more faithful in their stewardship.

Planning becomes more than a routine responsibility as people, organizations, and churches experience change. If everything stayed the same, we would know what to do in the future because it would look like the past. But in the face of change happening around us, we have to explore the alternatives that present themselves as possible ways to focus our energies in the days and years ahead. Those alternatives keep raising questions of purpose.

Church planning takes on its greatest urgency, however, as evangelism becomes difficult. That happens among churches that had an infectious spirit of witness and growth but now find themselves getting little response when they tell the same story. Something has changed. The Lord is the same. The believers themselves probably have become more settled and selective in their sharing. Most likely the people they want to reach now have slight or even major changes in perspective from those who responded so well earlier. After years of frustration, many once-vibrant churches lose even the desire to spread the Good News, except perhaps in symbolic ways. The excitement has gone out of it for them.

Only the Holy Spirit can rekindle excitement about life in Christ. I will have much more to say about that later. Churches, however,

15

can prepare themselves for new movement of the Spirit among them. Hearing the Word of God's promise of new life is basic. Serious planning is also part of such preparation. That begins where Jesus began, with the question: "What are we seeking?" It continues with a church's exploration of where, how, and with whom Jesus is staying among people today.

What follows helps set the stage for a productive planning process, especially in old churches. This is not meant as a planning manual, of which many are available. Rather the focus is on two ingredients of good church planning that can help elevate an otherwise formal exercise into an exciting experience of renewed discipleship. One is asking leading questions that often do not come to mind, about how God is present today.The other is recognizing relevant alternatives for responding to Him that may be overlooked.

Evangelism flows from Jesus' challenge to "Come and see." Planning is a way for churches to go and look.

New church life can be studied as church growth. That effort has taken on an identity of its own, recognized by capitalizing the name Church Growth. My old church perspective is influenced by association with colleagues who are leaders in the Church Growth field. Along with underscoring commitment to the Biblical basis for outreach, Church Growth stresses the discipleship responsibility to plan and manage a church's outreach. Planning for church growth forces attention on effectiveness, which is often not a dominant concern among those who stress historical faithfulness. Evangelicalism is a fitting environment to study how churches grow, because in fact most of the growth in American Christianity in recent decades has been among Evangelical expressions of the church.

The next chapter will suggest two distinctions that are helpful for guiding a church's planning for evangelism. One is to determine whether its goal is to build that church as a temple or a tabernacle. The other is to determine whether possible alternatives would affect the style that a church can consider changing or endanger the substance that a church has to preserve. Planning assesses risk of success or failure, and the third chapter will make some suggestions about how churches can look at success theologically. That is important for focusing a compelling vision that is a prerequisite for doing evangelism and church planning well.

FOLLOWING A MOBILE AND VERSATILE LORD

If the Lord's leading question points to a response of planning, the disciples' leading question points to a Lord who stands beyond our ability to confine Him to our plans. Even though He was with them, He was going to be somewhere else, too, and they did not know where.

Members of old churches can be helped to regain an infectious spirit for their evangelism by remembering that they follow a mobile and versatile Lord. When we look at where Jesus is staying now, we have to recognize that all His people make up a growing worldwide church that is wondrously diverse. As near as we can tell, Jesus is staying today with about one billion people who consider themselves to be Christians. He has moved considerably beyond the lands of His historic followers—first from the Mediterranean world a long time ago to Northern Europe, then to the Americas, and more recently with a powerful presence to Asia and Africa. His disciples share the Gospel in hundreds of languages, and they respond in daily lives that are shaped by societies and cultures that are vastly different.

What are we to make of this competence of our Lord, who can be so mobile and versatile? Clearly He is the leader and the rest of us are the followers. Lest any gathering of His disciples forget and try to confine Him to what they understand and want to do, He shows up somewhere else, generating new responses to His leadership. When we want to define limits, He reminds us again and again that He is a God of possibilities. To reach out to a world that is constantly changing, He is quite capable of causing and blessing fruitful change somewhere in His church. "Watch it happen" is a meaning contained in the challenge to "Come and see."

Lutherans have a long memory as they watch God's church happen. This is what makes theirs an old church. They value their history highly and believe they have much to preserve. They are a confessional church, which means Lutherans take the substance of their theology very seriously. Such history and theology are great strengths to be shared.

But the strength can also become a weakness, when this rich past shapes a preference to look backward while trying to follow Christ forward. Other old churches as well have weaknesses that

17

revolve around a hesitance to energetically probe unsettling questions of the future and a reluctance to explore new alternatives that depart from established ways.

In America today many of the new alternatives that merit attention are emerging in Evangelical churches. While all Protestant denominations began as a reform or renewal movement, the Evangelical memory of the burst of new life that brought those churches together is typically measured more in decades than centuries. Evangelism remains a driving concern for almost all of them. Short histories and a strong sense of purpose often result in a greater openness to innovation and adaptation of ministry styles than longer established church bodies can sustain. The leading questions of the Evangelicals are more on the side of how best to accomplish future-oriented goals of bringing Christ to others than in the direction of how to be faithful to past-oriented church patterns among those who are already Christians. Evangelicalism offers a lively environment for exploring new alternatives for following a mobile and versatile Lord.

QUESTIONS FOR OLD CHURCHES

I want to address the questions asked by leaders who are trying to think through a responsible course of action for their old church's future ministry in an American society and church scene that is shifting around them.

In the face of alternatives, the right first question is, What can we learn? Then can come the question, What can we change, if anything? Not to be forgotten is the question, What can we share to strengthen the ministry of others?

Those questions unavoidably raise others. This is so especially for churches that want to follow a mobile and versatile Lord while treasuring the unique history of His past actions among them. Is He really calling them to look at a new and different future for themselves, or is He choosing to stay among them as they have been? What is the course of faithfulness in mixing innovation and preservation? Where is the dividing line between laudable adaptation of outreach style and necessary protection of unchangeable theological substance? When does acceptance of the complicated responsibility to recognize and choose among alternatives turn into avoidance of the simple responsibility to obey? What does it mean when the Lord no longer grants growth to some church bodies but does to others, particularly those that have less allegiance to historic patterns of church life? How important is church growth?

If the following chapters serve their purpose, individual churches and pastors will have even more questions to consider for their own ministry. But there are suggestions for answers, too. They are meant for discussion among those who are open to looking at their historic church style in different ways. The best answers are those that members of a church arrive at with confidence that their discipleship is faithful to their Lord.

Ultimately, the Holy Spirit has to create an infectious evangelistic spirit among a gathering of believers. Jesus' challenge to "Come and see" where He is staying today can prepare churches for fresh movement of the Holy Spirit among them.

CHAPTER 2

Concentrating on the Adiaphora of Style

The early church leaders struggled with issues of old church and new styles. Peter, Paul, James, and Stephen had important things to say about innovation and preservation. They were helping God give birth to the new church of their time. What became the Christian church then is still preserved as the Christian church now, but many, many innovations happened during the centuries in between.

Watching how God chose to move among people in new ways brought those first leaders to the necessity of figuring out new ways to react. Their reasoning can be helpful to old churches as they react to new movement today. As the Book of Acts relates, change brought confusion amidst excitement and fear. Those disciples found insight for their course of action by making some fundamental distinctions. It will be helpful to translate those distinctions into the current language of planning and strategy.

Stephen knew firsthand the turmoil innovation brings to people who are used to following God in long-established ways. It cost him his life. Just before his martyrdom he saw with clarity the necessity for God's church to retain identity as a tabernacle. The contrast is a temple. His message is in Acts 7. We can distinguish between a temple or a tabernacle strategy today.

Paul of course was a remarkable church growth innovator. His effectiveness brought tension into the first established Christian church, which within several decades already had some tendencies to concentrate on preservation. Peter and James spoke up at the planning council that was convened to set a strategy for adjusting to unanticipated change. The account is in Acts 15. Their strategy enabled them to distinguish between what could change and what had to remain the same. That distinction remains a fundamental starting point for church planning today.

SUBSTANCE AND STYLE

The reasoning used by the Jerusalem planning council can be understood in the categories of substance and style. I propose those categories as a helpful distinction for old churches considering new approaches to evangelism. The categories are especially familiar to translators who have to be sure of the substantive meaning presented first in one language and its culture and then in another language and its culture. The words change, but the meaning should stay the same.

Congregations or church bodies have as their substance the part of their identity that has to remain unchanged. Style can be identified as how a church expresses that substance. Style can and does change over the years, just as languages and cultures do. Adopting new styles of church expression amounts to adapting to changes in cultures.

Singing a 16th-century hymn led by a pipe organ or repeating simple refrains to the strumming of a guitar would be considered a matter of style by most churches. Beliefs about who Jesus is and what He did are clearly substance. Each church has its own way of formulating the additional matters of substance that become for those believers the cause for their existence as an organized church. Each also has its own distinctive style that evolves out of those believers expressing themselves in their particular circumstances.

Substance is not subject to planning. Style is. Style can be recognized primarily in the way church people communicate what they believe and do and in the ways churches organize to sustain themselves and to carry out their work. Wide diversity in such matters is evident among American Protestants today. Evangelicals in particular have developed styles that differ from those usually seen in historic mainline churches today.

Styles of church life do seem related to church growth. Southern Baptists, for instance, have maintained a consistent and impressive rate of growth in recent decades. One can readily observe a worship style in such a church that is very different from a traditional liturgical service like that of Lutherans. Their style of organizing is

21

quite different from that of Presbyterians. Pentecostals like the Assemblies of God have characteristic worship and organizational styles that are different in yet other ways, and they have experienced one of the fastest rates of growth of any American church body.

Saying that style is the cause of growth is an oversimplification. The study of church growth reveals the complexity of cause-and-effect relationships, as much as these can be understood by human observers. Clearly theological substance remains a basic factor. That was pointed out well by Dean Kelly in his analysis of why conservative churches are growing, as noted in the Introduction. But style is also a factor. Recognizing how is important, particularly in view of the changes in American culture that are affecting style.

Concentrating on style makes the challenge of following a mobile and versatile Lord easier for churches. It is very difficult for one church to have enough respect for another's difference in substance to accept insights that modify its self-understanding of faithful discipleship. But there is latitude for changes in styles of talking and organizing. How one church responds to new and different social circumstances can provide helpful insights to other churches trying to cope with similar situations.

For most churches the line between style and substance remains unclearly drawn. The effort to reestablish it again and again remains necessary for churches that expect to continue a lively ministry among people living in different and changing cultures. Serious pursuit of the planning process forces that effort. Because its starting point is change, planning itself is most faithful when done in the context of a theology confident of what does not change.

For some Lutherans there may be a question whether liturgical worship belongs to their substance. They would resist treating it as style, as implied earlier. But in fact Lutheran worship practice has considerable variance and has had that over the centuries. For Lutherans, substance revolves around beliefs, which are readily identified in the Confessions that define Lutheranism. The Confessions recognize considerable latitude in matters of practice and thereby in style. The conceptual term for what is at issue here is "adiaphora"—things which God neither commands nor forbids and which therefore are subject to human judgment. Planning is a process of applying such judgment to adiaphora. It can and should facilitate changes in style.

THE APOSTLES' EVANGELISM STRATEGY

We can learn about sorting out substance and style from the very first Christian planning council. It was convened in Jerusalem. Out of it came a planning strategy that can guide evangelism today.

The story begins in Acts 15 with recognition that the Lord is indeed mobile and versatile. Through the missionary work of Paul and Barnabas, He was staying with new people in new lands, and also in new ways. While the older Christians were "very glad" at what they heard (Acts 15:3–4), some from the home base in Jerusalem resisted the changes they saw happening in their church. They were followers of the Messiah who attached great importance to maintaining their Jewish customs and life-style. They had what today could be called an ethnic church. The newest Christians had come to faith as they were, and they lived their life in Christ differently. They were Gentiles, people from other cultures and nations. To be true Christians, did they have to follow the customs of the Jews, especially circumcision? Was that part of the substance?

That first council emerged to address this question. The early church had to work out a plan, an agreement on principles they would use in facing the future. We know that Paul, Barnabas, Peter, and James were part of the council, along with other apostles and elders. They saw a need to support those who were following Christ in new ways. They accepted the responsibility to be stewards of the resources for new life God had left them. They were willing to sort out and clarify their God-given goals. In today's vocabulary, we could say they had gathered to settle on a strategy, which is a long-range plan for committing resources to meet specified needs in order to accomplish explicit goals.

The need they chose was to support those other Christians by removing as many obstacles as they could for the new life God had started among them. In the summary of the council president, James, God at first showed His concern for these people, and "we should not make it difficult for the Gentiles who are turning to God" (vv. 14, 19). As Peter saw it, they should refrain from testing God by putting any unnecessary yoke on the neck of those disciples (v. 10). Peter was very conscious of their responsibility to interpret the church's response to God's act of purifying hearts by faith (v. 9). They were stewards of "the grace of our Lord Jesus" (v. 11).

James presented the goal for their strategy. He held out the vision, expressed by the prophet Amos, of following the God who wants His church to be built up and to grow ("I will ... rebuild David's fallen tent"), so that His original people and all others who bear His name may seek Him (vv. 17–18). The council's dominant goal, therefore, would be to build for the future, not just to preserve what was customary among them. They clarified what they were seeking.

This strategy of removing obstacles to growth by relying on God's grace determined their response to the issue at hand. Those leaders agreed to maximize the scope for fitting the Christian life to the different cultural styles and expectations of these new believers. They would do this by paring down to the bare minimum what was necessary to sustain discipleship in the church that was changing around them. As the minutes of the meeting state, "It seemed good to the Holy Spirit and to us not to burden you with anything beyond the following requirements" (v. 28).

DRAWING A LINE

What these leaders did is to draw a line between substance and style. Some had wanted to make circumcision part of the unchanging substance of the church. Others among the new Gentile Christians apparently thought most of the Jewish piety was just a matter of style that did not apply to their situation. The conclusion was that most indeed was style, but a few practices still belonged to the substance of that church: "You are to abstain from food sacrificed to idols, from blood, from the meat of strangled animals and from sexual immorality" (v. 29).

Christians today may find this a rather odd list. Avoiding sexual immorality remains a substance mandate. But keeping food kosher ("abstain from ... blood [and] the meat of strangled animals") is hardly even a style concern anymore for Christians, who have long ago abandoned that constraint. Avoiding food sacrificed to idols might be debated if the question arose, but few Christians today live in a culture where that circumstance arises.

Clearly the early Christians recognized more to be of substance than this short list. Apparently they assumed the best of people who professed Jesus as Lord. They chose to concentrate only on those matters that were causing difficulty at a time of change.

What we can observe from this first council is that the line between church substance and style can and does shift. For that time and place, they had to make a decision about what they could let change and what they had to preserve. Line-drawing decisions have been made again and again over the centuries of changed circumstances encountered by God's people. As they encountered exciting but threatening innovation, even the early Christians had to maintain integrity with their unique history. Significantly, it was the mission enterprise to new people that caused the tension. Following the Christ would have been easier for the Jerusalem Jews without Paul's innovations that were showing themselves to be so effective in church growth.

So also today, it is mission and evangelism efforts that regularly introduce tension into church life by trying to relate the Gospel to people different from those already there. Each church or church body has its own version of the Jerusalem Jewish Christians who feel the responsibility to preserve what has been important in their history. The tension is necessary. So is the will to seek accommodation between the forces for innovation and those for preservation.

The Acts story gives us a model for how to do that. Recognize and celebrate new life where it occurs. Confront the tension with the old directly in an open council where the opposing concerns can be heard. Then be willing to draw the line as consciously and sensibly as possible, but do so with the determination to burden no follower with more than is necessary. Keep central the goal of building the church. Above all, listen to the Lord, so that the conclusion can be announced as it was then: It seems good to the Holy Spirit and to us that we be ready to accept these certain changes but that we hold these other matters to be unchanging.

THE GOAL CONFUSION STEPHEN SAW

Stephen's ministry gives us another Biblical contribution to evangelism planning. He contributed a distinction between seeing God's presence in a temple or a tabernacle. Stephen did not define the difference. He just used it to explain how God's people should react to God's movement of His presence.

Significantly, Stephen was an administrator who concentrated on helping the church turn its intentions into realities in everyday living. His primary task of organizing the distribution of the Christian community's food resources must have kept him close to the church planning process. Apparently it also heightened his sensitivity to goals for an emerging strategy of church life. Facing his martyrdom, he clarified where he saw the Lord staying and what the church was supposed to do, as recorded in his testimony in Acts 7.

According to Stephen, the people of God were at their best when they were most conscious of following a God who kept moving on. The Lord's challenge to come and see was issued to Abraham in the words, "Leave your country and your people ... and go to the land I will show you" (Acts 7:3). Stephen is very careful to describe in detail how the followers stayed on the move under Joseph, Moses, Joshua, and even David. The symbol of their intent to stay mobile was the tabernacle: "Our forefathers had the tabernacle of the Testimony with them in the desert" (v. 44). The tabernacle was the portable sanctuary carried by the Israelites on their wanderings. It was really a tent.

The goal for God's people got confused when Solomon replaced the tent with a temple (v. 47). That shift led to Stephen's main point: "However, the Most High does not live in houses made by men" (v. 48). The church gets its goals wrong when followers think God stays where they prefer to put Him. Even after Solomon that was clear, as the Lord said through Isaiah: "Heaven is my throne and earth is my footstool. What kind of house will you build for me? says the Lord. Or where will my resting place be? Has not my hand made all these things?" (vv. 49–50).

Note here that our God again teaches His people with questions. He will not let us escape the necessity to ask ourselves what we think we are doing in our churchly discipleship.

Stephen wraps up his message on facing the future with a negative statement of the important goal: "You always resist the Holy Spirit!" (v. 51). The new church is to remain open to the Spirit. It is the Holy Spirit today who continually shows believers how God has moved on and where He is staying now. It is the Holy Spirit who helps the followers see where their Lord is and how they can stay with Him in new lands and cultures.

From the same John who tells us about Jesus' challenge to "Come and see" we also know what it means to stay open to the

Spirit, who shows us the way. Despite our every effort to pin God down to predictable expressions of His presence, the Holy Spirit acts like the wind that "blows wherever it pleases. You hear its sound, but you cannot tell where it comes from or where it is going" (John 3:8).

A TEMPLE OR A TABERNACLE STRATEGY?

Properly understood, the temple can remain a helpful planning image for Christian churches. It focuses attention on permanence. But Stephen's message forces churches today to interpret that permanence as something they themselves cannot build or preserve. For old churches today, the question is whether they will emphasize efforts to regard their church as a temple or whether they will stress what makes them a mobile tabernacle.

The temple imagery remains compelling for Christians. No less a church builder than the tent-maker Paul placed it firmly in the vocabulary of Christ's followers: "For we are the temple of the living God," he said. "As God has said: 'I will live with them and walk among them, and I will be their God, and they will be my people'" (2 Cor 6:16). The temple is not to be destroyed (1 Cor 3:17); it is to be honored (1 Cor 6:19–20).

In terms of substance and style, we can think of the temple part of church life as the anchoring of the Lord's presence in His unchanging purpose and will for His people. His actions and declarations that He is our God and we are His people are the substance. Like an immovable temple, that God-given core of a Christian community's existence is to be protected and honored as well as we know how.

The church as tabernacle is recognition of God's presence that changes. Like a portable tent, He can stay with His people wherever they are and under whatever circumstances they are living, in ways they can see, understand, and respond to as they are. The tabernacle aspect of the church is God's ability to adapt His presence to the specific style of church life His followers have to develop in order to remain faithful in the social and cultural conditions that shape their daily living. As cultures change or people come to faith in different societies, churches as tabernacles move along, learning new styles of keeping God's presence visible in changed circumstances.

A faithful church of Christ needs to be both temple and tabernacle. The question is which part to emphasize in planning for the future. Some churches choose to pursue mostly what can be called a temple strategy. Others are more inclined to a tabernacle strategy.

The strategy of the "planning council" in Jerusalem emphasized the church as tabernacle. That was made explicit in James' goal statement that looked for the Lord to return and rebuild David's fallen *tent*. The reason was so that all the different people of the world could seek the Lord and see His presence (Acts 15:16–17). Confronting the diversity that comes with growth, those first church leaders concentrated on how God could accept and bless many different styles of honoring Him. The tabernacle equips a mission strategy.

A temple strategy often emerges for a church in times of adversity and judgment, when believers are unsure of their distinctiveness in the Lord. Then the goal of preservation becomes dominant. The human need to be addressed is for assurance and certainty of God's unchanging presence and promise. The church resource is remembrance and celebration of fixed points in history where God was visibly active among those followers, making His glory known and defining their identity as His chosen people. Each church or church body can add to the Biblical base its own unique history of God's memorable actions in their midst. Sometimes the blessing of having a large or unusual sanctuary serves to anchor such a testimony. Emphasizing the preservation of a church's history, or traditions, or institutions can become a temple orientation that enables a church to say, "We know who we are because of this visible, fixed point of our attention."

The early church leaders understood temple thinking very well. They lived in the shadow of the ultimate temple on earth, the physical building in Jerusalem and all the preserved ceremonies centered there. This very visible point of reference, however, made them particularly sensitive to the dangers associated with using this image to understand what Christians are to seek. Instead of being a place to see the living God at work, a temple can become only a man-made artifact that no longer holds a God whose Spirit has moved on to other places. Followers of Christ need to be careful lest they try to preserve the wrong thing.

Paul's use of the temple image is a necessary reminder to churches that want to build temples that stay the same. He used it to describe God's presence in people, individually (1 Cor. 6:19) or together as God's living church (2 Cor 6:16). The temple is God's people, in whom His Spirit lives (1 Cor. 3:16). Paul did not speak of it as a historical or fixed point of reference that exists apart from the live people God is staying with at the time. The temple is not the traditions, understandings, accomplishments, or institutions any church builds. Where and how God chooses to call people His own, there is the temple to be honored and guarded. But because God keeps moving on, the temple of God's current presence is better thought of as a tabernacle.

Later I will suggest the image of a camp to convey the sense of a church as a temporary gathering of believers ready to move on. Quite literally, camp events, such as revivals, were the formative experience of many Evangelical churches, and the demands of evangelizing and initiating church life in this setting explain much of the style Evangelicals developed. The contrast is the stable village setting that was most formative for Lutheran style.

The important question will be whether the people to be reached with the Gospel in America today live more in villagelike settings where they expect to have firm, well-established social roots, or whether camplike living has become more the norm, with people sharing little common history and expecting to make few long-term commitments. The answer is full of implications for style of church life. In any event, because they are more accustomed to experiencing church in temporary settings, Evangelicals are more prone to see God's presence in the form of a movable tabernacle. This orientation adds significance to their style.

There are times when church leaders may have good cause to emphasize a temple strategy. Given the centuries-long history of the changing Christian church, however, they are in for a surprise if they regard those times as anything more than refortification periods for future adaptations to the new life God will send in unexpected ways. Jesus had significant things to say about the futility of efforts His followers might expend trying on their own to preserve what is important to them. We need to look at that in the next chapter.

CHAPTER 3

From the Cross to
a New Vision

Martin Luther featured the theology of the cross. He loved to cite Jesus' words, "If anyone would come after me, he must deny himself and take up his cross and follow me" (Mark 8:34). Here we have a lesson on the challenge to come and see about how to follow Jesus.

For Luther the theology of the cross stood in contrast to a theology of glory. Christians are prone to the latter when they want to evaluate their discipleship according to the results or glory it brings. Triumphalism is another (negative) word for an approach to church life that encourages people to follow Christ because of the visible triumphs He will bring to their lives.

Advocates of church planning can be accused of practicing a theology of glory. Church Growth as a movement may be guilty of triumphalism, according to worries of many pastors who know their Luther. The concentration on results raises those concerns, especially when church leaders who explore alternatives are encouraged to settle on one because "it works" for their situation. When Jesus said "Come and see," was He just telling us to look for what works? The theology of the cross would seem to suggest otherwise.

Far from negating an effort to go and look, however, such theology is necessary preparation for faithful church planning and God-pleasing church growth. The meaning of the cross is the theological starting point. That is true for churches as well as for individuals. Living the way of the cross makes it possible for churches to recognize success and to make the choices that help them continue to bring it about.

Jesus challenged those first disciples to "Come and see" because He wanted to give them a new vision. He gives churches new visions, too. New evangelism styles for old churches will emerge as they find the new vision that God will use to energize their outreach. New visions are the key to regaining an infectious church spirit. But that is possible only when the cross is taken seriously.

THE CROSS AS PREPARATION

The cross can be a symbol of suffering. With that as the point of reference, to follow means to suffer. I have talked with many pastors who seem to regard the suffering of their old church as a badge of faithfulness. This comes out in discussions of declining membership or waning support for established stances and programs. The cross becomes a source of comfort to explain what is happening to them. They see the Lord testing their faithfulness. For some, the theology of the cross means they should simply continue what they are doing and avoid exploring alternatives lest the suffering be reduced by greater success.

I do not think this is what Jesus had in mind when He urged His followers to take up their cross. As Jesus knew so well, the cross was an instrument of death. To deny yourself means much more than to deny your ambitions by learning to suffer. With the cross as symbol of death, He meant for His followers to deny any dependence on themselves, to put to death all vestiges of their personal history and past accomplishments that would cause them to have anything less than total dependence on the One they are following into the future. This is clear in His explanation: "For whoever wants to save his life will lose it, but whoever loses his life for me and for the gospel will save it" (Mark 8:35). To live by the cross is to live totally by faith.

Believers who deny themselves to follow Jesus are ready to live a life of risks. This modern word can serve partially to translate the meaning of the cross into a church's understanding of the issue of preservation vs. innovation. Risk is a measurement of how much someone is willing to lose. Some churches can contemplate losing their life in the abstract but in practice seem very intent on trying to save it. Their style revolves around reducing risks to the continuance of faithful ministry. This is a tendency among older churches like mine that remember a long history of dangers. Other, newer churches often seem oblivious to the risks to which they expose

31

their Gospel ministry, sometimes with striking naïveté. Yet God grants them growth.

THE MEASURE OF SUCCESS

The way of the cross is especially difficult for older churches. God can save them only when they are willing to lose their own unique life with its preserved memories and protected style. Why should they take that risk? As Jesus said, for His sake and the Gospel's. Translated for churches into a current popular term, we can say that churches should deny themselves and go the way of the cross—for the sake of success. Of course, that is success as God defines it, not as organizations measure it. Success begins with crucifying dependence on ourselves. But that is really a means to a larger end. As Jesus said in completing His saying on following Him, the purpose is to "see the kingdom of God come with power" (Mark 9:1). God's kingdom is His presence among people, taking charge of their lives and using His power to change them.

"Watch Me do that!" is what Jesus was saying to those first disciples when He told them to "Come and see" where He was staying. "Deny yourself . . . and follow me" means to let Him use His disciples as He wills in order to help the kingdom of God come over and over again among the people of the world. Denial itself is not the measure of success. The coming of the kingdom is.

As churches today try to identify the course Jesus calls them to follow, they have to ask themselves where He is staying now, that is, where the kingdom of God is coming with power. To be faithful, they have to be ready to let themselves be used for such Kingdom work, when and where God does it. This means remaining open to the Holy Spirit's movement among them. For older churches such following means asking when the effort to preserve traditional practices and doctrinal formulations interferes with dependence on the Lord who alone can grant life and understanding in the future. Where is the point where their church building effort turns into temple avoidance of the risks of tabernacle living?

Church growth should not be suspect. It can only happen where the kingdom of God comes with power. When some churches grow more than others, that has to be God's choice. He is able to use those churches in special ways. Often that is because He is bringing

His power to bear on people who live in specialized circumstances, customizing His presence among them. Sometimes He chooses to have His kingdom come with fresh power for new responses among those with whom He has dwelt for a long time. Those are His choices.

CHURCH CHOICES

Each church also has choices. A community of believers can stay constantly on the alert for new signs of the Kingdom around them, or they can concentrate only on preserving what they have seen of God's presence so far. When God grants growth elsewhere, church leaders can resolve to learn more about the style of ministry He is using so well, or they can feel disappointed that He is not working more energetically through styles they already know how to provide. When God visibly blesses their own life in Christ, they can try to capture His presence in a temple of fixed traditions they resolve to repeat, or, strengthened by that experience, they can expect to keep their tabernacle on the move as the Kingdom comes with power in new ways.

Jesus' followers face choices day after day and year after year. Gathered as a church, they consciously or unconsciously develop strategies to give a pattern to those choices. It is not inappropriate to ask if the particular pattern of goals, needs, and resources they emphasize is continuing to bring success. That is, how well is God able to use them to bring His kingdom with power among the people they touch? Are there other things they could do that would make them better instruments? What are the alternatives? Where is Jesus now as He says, "Come and see."

Like other people, Christians tend to avoid hard decisions, and their churches can get used to strategies they no longer consciously recognize or examine. That is why some sort of deliberate planning process becomes so important. This effort focuses attention on the hard questions, the exploration of alternatives, and then the intentional making of difficult decisions.

Planning itself will not bring success. But it can help a church make the changes that put it on a course the Lord can better use for the success of His efforts. As pastors and church leaders well know, churches are continually risking their existence and the unique history, identity, and style they offer. That can be for the simple reason of the human weaknesses that affect any organization. Faithful church planning, however, aims at deliberately risking a church's familiar life-style for the right reasons of discipleship. Then God can give new life for such a church's future stewardship.

A NEW VISION

Effective evangelism and church planning both share a common prerequisite. Those making the effort have to be moved by a vision of a different and better future they are seeking. They have to have aspirations, or a dream that pulls them forward.

Visions and dreams were prominent in the motivation of the apostles. At Pentecost, Peter explained their obvious enthusiasm by quoting from the prophet Joel: "In the last days, God says, I will pour out my Spirit on all people. Your sons and daughters will prophesy, your young men will see visions, and your old men will dream dreams" (Acts 2:17).

In the Biblical culture, visions and dreams were regarded as special perceptions of God's presence and will. In our modern culture we talk more about a vision as an image of the future we can join together to bring about, and a dream as an ambition to be achieved. Christians can combine both meanings in their church life. Thinking about what might happen in the future, a church can have a dream of specific ways the kingdom of God could come more powerfully through its fellowship and witness. A new vision is what disciples might find after they go and look at other ways Jesus can stay among people and thus among them, too. Getting that vision is a good reason to take up Jesus' challenge, "Come and see."

The desire to explore, however, is usually reduced in churches that try to move themselves with old visions, as old churches often do. Then the dream becomes little more than maintaining what they have already accomplished. Maintenance ministries are important, but they typically do not generate infectious excitement. It is a vision of some new life God is about to give that quickens the desire for evangelism into an infectious evangelistic spirit. The need for a new vision, and for the exploration to find it, is most clearly recognized as it becomes difficult simply to maintain the old one. Ultimately,

God gives churches a new vision. Their histories show how He does it. While He works through gifted leaders, God prepares the people by making the need for some sort of change apparent.

AN EXAMPLE

Just about every surviving old congregation or church body can illustrate out of their history how God periodically grants a new vision. I know the process best through the history of my own church. I offer that as an example.

The Lord gave The Lutheran Church—Missouri Synod a new vision a number of times in its history. The church was born from change. Its first necessary vision was to build new congregations among the German immigrants to the Midwest who had left the old country in the mid 1800s. Among those people, this church body had an infectious spirit, especially under the leadership of C. F. W. Walther. When outreach was hampered because there were not enough pastors and teachers, a second generation dreamed of building institutions to train more of them. The synod founded most of its colleges for that purpose toward the end of the century.

Whereas a new land prepared these Lutheran Christians for new visions in the 19th century, a new language provided that stimulus through much of the 20th. The First World War spelled an end to the dream of a church that would keep Christ visible through the style of a German culture on American soil. Becoming effective at witnessing (and worshiping) in the English language was a new compelling vision. The radio ministry of the Lutheran Hour ("Bringing Christ to the Nations"), starting in the 1930s, expressed the dream of a national evangelistic impact, and many Missouri Synod congregations today still remember that excitement by publicly identifying themselves as The Church of the Lutheran Hour.

The new vision that emerged for the synod in the 1950s and '60s is too recent to be summarized with clarity. I can offer an interpretation as seen through my participation in the excitement. I think we were still propelled by the stimulus of adapting new styles that were to help move our outreach beyond the confines of the separatist ways associated with the old language. The significant increase in the general level of higher education among Lutherans after World War II also presented evident expectations for changes in style of ministry. Part of the dream was to become more accul-turated into the mainline of American religious life. Many in the church were excited by a vision of liturgical renewal and its more consistently content-rich, polished worship.

In the 1970s the then-dominant new visions were dramatically challenged through major conflict within the church body. With so much change in style, that became a time for the church to redefine substance. Significantly, in a period of still finishing the transition to the new language and its culture, the central issue was the Word of God and its authority. The result of the painful doctrinal and institutional battles in that decade is that this church body firmly drew a line to preserve its unchangeable theological substance.

What is the new vision now? In the late 1980s that is not yet apparent. Simply recovering from conflict and healing the wounds was a necessary short-term vision. The effort to redefine substance aroused in many a dream of reclaiming former style, too. But that may be an old vision that does not excite a widespread burst of new life and evangelistic spirit. Indeed there is mounting evidence of the need for a compelling new vision. Church membership is not growing. Denominational programs are still in a period of re-trenchment, and a number of denominational institutions are strug-gling to survive. Many who care deeply about their church find it harder to spot the new life that brings infectious growth.

God will almost assuredly grant this church a new vision that propels it into a new burst of growth. There is no guarantee, though. He has let other church bodies decline to the point of death. As a mobile and versatile Lord, He does move on. The current task for this church is to seek and be open to the vision of how He wants to use it to help His kingdom come with power in a society and world that continue to change. This is a church that has just been through a necessary time of temple orientation toward preservation. A new vision will come if that was only a temporary period and the church is ready to resume the journey of following Him with its tabernacle of His presence.

COME AND SEE

"Come and see," Jesus says. The vision can emerge as believers go and look. What old churches should look for is styles of church life through which He most readily stays with people in today's culture around us. To be gained are insight and enthusiasm for how to continue changing their own distinctive styles.

No one can know if a forceful new vision for an old church will emerge from looking at how Jesus is staying with the newer, Evangelical churches. The fact that God is granting visible growth among many of them is reason enough to look. To become exactly like some other church should not be the intent. That would be unfaithful stewardship of His past, unique blessings to an old church. Rather, the purpose should be to learn new possibilities for sharing the strengths inherited from that past.

In the following chapters I see myself offering a scouting report on Evangelical church vitality. Part II offers an analysis of the lay of the land. These chapters concentrate on recognizing the diversity to be seen and on describing how that relates to old churches. They emphasize Lutheranism. Part III suggests shifts in emphasis that can be considered in styles of communicating and organizing.

Evangelism can take on an infectious spirit only through the movement of the Holy Spirit. But a church's style shapes its experience of the Spirit. Through an openness to changing styles, old churches can experience the Holy Spirit in new ways that indeed bring an infectious evangelistic spirit.

PART 2

Seeing and Assessing Evangelical Styles

Introduction

"Come and see" is the invitation Christians extend in their evangelism. We considered these words as a challenge from Jesus to His followers. Now we should repeat them as our words to others. Philip said those words to Nathanael, as the Gospel of John relates a few verses after Jesus' encounter with the first disciples (John 1:46).

How do we make that an invitation which engages and attracts people today? One author recognizes three general evangelism styles:[1]

1. A content-oriented approach. The invitation amounts to communicating basic facts which the hearer needs to know. The Christian is like a teacher to someone who is the student. The evangelism strategy has the goal of imparting correct information.

2. A confrontation-oriented approach. This approach stresses the right persuasive technique to get someone to "Come and see." The evangelist is like a salesman appealing to a customer. The goal is to close the "sale."

3. A relationship-oriented approach. The intent is to share the Gospel message in personal relationships through which someone else can experience the assurance of God's love it conveys. The Christian seeks to relate to someone else as friend to friend. The goal is, through word and deed, to love the person as God does.

If we could go and look at which style is most effective among Americans today, what would we find? Flavil Yeakley made such an effort. Here is his report.

He identified over 700 people who had been "recipients" of an evangelistic presentation, and he divided them into three equal-sized groups according to (a) those who made a Christian commitment and stayed active in a local church, (b) those who made a commitment and soon dropped out, and (c) those who said "no thanks" at the outset.

Yeakley found that: (1) By far the most (75%) of those who did not respond did so in reaction to evangelism that seemed simply

41

the sharing of content and facts. (2) By far the most (87%) of those who made an initial commitment but dropped out had come through the effort of a church member whose evangelism was "confrontational." (3) By far most (70%) of those who stayed active in their new church viewed themselves as approached through evangelism that can be characterized as "relational."[2]

Styles of evangelism do make a difference. These findings would imply that churches whose approach is today seen as just sharing the correct information about their faith are most in need of learning new styles. The findings would also imply that churches should concentrate on learning more about the approach that is most associated with facilitating an initial and longer-term commitment to a fellowship of believers.

In their practice of evangelism Lutherans historically have relied on the content-oriented approach. Their greatest growth occurred among people who were willing students for careful teaching. The current lack of growth suggests that the people to be reached are not such deferential students anymore. It is important to recognize what has happened.

Evangelical churches are often regarded as relying on the confrontational approach. Many stress the importance of "making a decision for Christ." That approach is attractive. It can bring quick and sometimes dramatic results. Indeed, in many church circles, evangelism has almost become synonymous with confrontation. Christians can become better at it by learning new and improved techniques.

If Lutherans want to do evangelism more effectively today, should they look at confrontational approaches? Are those the new styles they should try to learn? Perhaps. But the implications need to be assessed, particularly in view of the substance of Lutheran theology. Chapter 6 presents some criteria for such assessment, which Chapter 7 will apply. Looking at this whole question needs to be done with one eye on Biblical insights and the other on effectiveness. I will draw on the analogy of marketing rather than sales as a human reference point for evaluating evangelistic outreach.

Evangelical and Lutheran styles can converge best on the third, relational approach. "Infectious" is a relational term, and an infectious spirit can best be regained by concentrating on this approach.

I see relation-oriented outreach as the real key to the growth of Evangelical churches. Its importance is suggested by research the Institute of American Church Growth did on the "love quotient" of various denominations. They did their looking with a 17-question Loving/Caring Quotient Survey of 8,600 respondents in 39 different denominations. They report a direct relationship between the rating of their friendliness and the growth of their denomination. The growing and "loving" denominations turned out to be Evangelical in orientation.[3]

From the viewpoint of those who are reached, a relational approach offers the experience of love and acceptance. Evangelism strives to anchor that in God's love and His promise of acceptance. But the words communicate through experience. Lutherans historically are wary of featuring experience. Yet for those who belong, the style of their church life historically has conveyed strong, lasting experiences of acceptance. Now some of the cultural prerequisites for the effectivensss of that style are fading, as I will explain. One result is that Lutherans score near the bottom on the Loving/Caring Quotient.

The place for Lutherans to look for new styles of evangelism is among churches that can communicate experiences of God-centered love and acceptance to people shaped by current cultures. Many newer Evangelical churches have found ways to do this, ways that can be borrowed. Lutherans, I suggest, can consider adapting some of those ways to their own style.

The process of borrowing styles needs to be understood, and Chapter 4 starts there.

CHAPTER 4

Styles of Evangelism

That there are good reasons for different styles of evangelism is apparent at the very beginning of Christian evangelism. Consider the different accounts of our Lord's parting words to His disciples at His ascension.

The evangelist Matthew's account is fundamental, of course, as presented in his 28th chapter. Significantly, we call it the Great Commission. Here are the familiar words:

> Then Jesus came to them and said, "All authority in heaven and on earth has been given to me. Therefore go and make disciples of all nations, baptizing them in the name of the Father and of the Son and of the Holy Spirit, and teaching them to obey everything that I have commanded you. And surely I am with you always, to the very end of the age" (Matt. 28:18–20).

Matthew is led to emphasize how Jesus left his followers with the command, "Go and make disciples of all nations." That this imperative is a command is even more apparent in the additional charge that we are to teach them to obey all that He commands. Through his encounter with God in Christ, Matthew was motivated to obey the instructions given him by his Commander. With him, we today continue the divinely appointed mission of extending to all people of the world what we know and believe.

The evangelist Luke's account is different, as presented in his 24th chapter. Here are his words, which are typically not quoted as often:

> Then he opened their minds so they could understand the Scriptures. He told them, "This is what is written: The Christ will suffer and rise from the dead on the third day, and repentance and forgiveness of sins will be preached in his name to all nations, beginning at Jerusalem. You are witnesses of these things. I am

44

going to send you what my Father has promised; but stay in the city, until you have been clothed with power from on high.

When he had led them out to the vicinity of Bethany, he lifted his hands and blessed them. While he vas blessing them, he left them and was taken up into heaven. Then they worshiped him and returned to Jerusalem with great joy. And they stayed continually in the temple, praising God (Luke 24:45–53)

The substance in Luke is the same, of course. But here the emphasis is not so much the command as the prediction. The verbs are without the imperative, as is evident in the Greek. Jesus left us with the promise that repentance and forgiveness will be preached in His name to all nations. We *will* be His witnesses; He does not say "should."

How we become His witnesses is significant. It is not so much by command as by being filled with power from on high. Luke is led to feature this prior action. Instead of going, as Matthew emphasizes, the disciples were to wait, to stay in the city, until God's power would come to them. For Luke it is apparent that the rest will take care of itself. He gives us a clue to how this will happen in the way he ends the story. The disciples went home with great joy and continually praised God.

We need not ask whether it is Matthew or Luke who is correct. They both are. My point is that they had different styles in expressing what the ascended Christ left for them to do. One focused on the God-given command to bring others to obedience. The other on the God-promised power to share their joy in Christ. Our Lord leaves us with both dimensions of evangelism today. I suggest that the emphasis on one or the other dimension explains much of the diversity in evangelism practices that we see in Christ's church today.

Christians must always heed the Great Commission passed on by Matthew. I think Luke's style, however, fits in better with historic Lutheranism. But today many other church bodies seem more adept at translating this motivation into action among Christ's followers. Lutherans have important theological reservations about how far we can go with that style, even though theirs has always been a style that emphasizes the life of joy and praise possible in Christ. Lutheran evangelism can be improved by finding new ways to receive the power from on high and to share the joy that flows from it.

APOSTOLIC BORROWING AT PENTECOST

The actual work of sharing that joy in Christ was done with borrowed styles right from the beginning of apostolic evangelism. The Pentecost event makes that clear. Significantly it is Luke who describes what happened, as told in the Book of Acts.

First Luke stresses that after their waiting the disciples were indeed clothed with power from on high:

> When the day of Pentecost came, they were all together in one place. Suddenly a sound like the blowing of a violent wind came from heaven and filled the whole house where they were sitting. They saw what seemed to be tongues of fire that separated and came to rest on each of them. All of them were filled with the Holy Spirit ... (Acts 2:1–4).

Thus God prepared them for what happened next. Through the Holy Spirit He gave them a spirit that became very infectious.

Their first response was to use unexpected styles of communication: "All ... began to speak in other tongues as the Spirit enabled them" (v. 4). In Jerusalem that day they faced people from many different national and cultural backgrounds. There were Parthians, Medes, Elamites, Egyptians, Cretans, Arabs, and so forth. Many ethnic groups are listed. Undoubtedly most could handle Hebrew or Greek as a second language. But what each group heard came in their primary tongue. Luke emphasizes this point. He remembers the people marveling that these men were Galileans, as they said, "How is it that each of us hears them in his own native language?" (2:8). According to the original text, what the people heard was their own "dialect." These unusual communication styles truly helped God's kingdom come with power that day. Three thousand were added to the company of disciples.

What was especially amazing is not only that the apostles spoke languages new to them but that they were enabled to master the subtleties of these specialized communications enough to have profound impact. Each group knew that message was meant for them. The first evangelists did not expect their audiences to hear the Gospel in the language and style that the apostles preferred. They adjusted to their different audiences. Open to the Spirit, the apostles were able to customize their message. They used many "borrowed" styles to proclaim the same substance.

Pentecost was a miracle, to be sure. But perhaps more important, it was a model—a model of how God will fulfill His promise to send the power by which the Gospel will be proclaimed to all nations. Through the Holy Spirit, God encourages and enables His disciples even today to communicate in the many different dialects appropriate to relating convincingly to people from all sorts of different cultural backgrounds.

Lutherans in America have been very effective at customizing their style to people who remember their European language and cultural roots. But the original audiences are changing and losing their ethnicity. That is partly the result of later-generation distance from the formative culture. It also comes as mobility and general cultural change take their toll on the established close-knit communities that appreciated historic Lutheran style.

As audiences change and diversify, the dialects for reaching them need also to change and diversify. To be sure, there is need for all American churches to learn more languages like Spanish and Chinese. But there is perhaps an even greater need, especially for older churches, to learn styles that use new subtleties of communicating within the growing cultural diversity of English-speaking Americans. As I will show, social changes point to a need to learn such new subtleties even when communicating the Gospel to the children of old-church believers.

It is exciting to think of the new styles to be learned as churches open themselves to the leading of the Spirit.

BORROWING CREATIVELY

Preparation for such movement by the Holy Spirit can seldom be done by mandate from a central headquarters. The new happens most effectively when it arises from the creative work of frontline church leaders who are freed up to customize their approach to the specialized social groupings around them.

Seeing the work of current frontline church builders is instructive. Dan Baumann went and looked. He makes his report in a book with the title *All Originality Makes a Dull Church*. Here he describes the mission strategy of nine well-known American churches. These include Coral Ridge Presbyterian Church, pastored by James Kennedy; Thomas Road Baptist Church, with Jerry Falwell; and Garden

Grove Community Church, led by Robert Schuler. He also offers his assessment of what makes the style of each of these effective church builders distinctive. Each church has an infectious spirit about it, a spirit that is contagious and attracts others who want to be part of it. Each church has a slightly different spirit (with a small s), with a creative blend of styles.

Baumann's title is important. He is borrowing Charles Spurgeon's advice that all originality and no borrowing makes dull preaching. Expanding that to church work, Baumann sees himself addressing pastors who expect to rely on their own ingenuity and creativity to develop the life and mission of their congregations. His advice is to rely a little more on insights and ideas gleaned from church builders whose approach is well blessed today. We can recast that advice as: Be more willing to incorporate into your own style of evangelism other styles shown to be effective today. Basic to Baumann's analysis is that each of the featured styles is a customized fit between the demographics and expectations of a given community and the leadership strengths of the pastor. Each style is original, although each borrows freely from those who have ministered the Gospel before.

The audience for Baumann's advice is Evangelical pastors. Lutheran church leaders are a different audience, with a different history. To customize his message, the blend he advocates could be better discovered by turning his advice around: All borrowing and no originality makes dull church work.

By tradition, Lutheran pastors are not prone to rely too much on their own ingenuity and creativity. I think they tend to rely too much on their borrowings, and they borrow from a very narrow pool of styles. For many reasons, some of which are related to history rooted in European state churches, Lutheran pastors are inclined to wait until someone tells them what emphases and programs to adopt. I do not want to suggest that there is now one best new style out there that should be found and officially approved. Rather, I would advocate that pastors be more original in developing a variety of styles of their own, customizing borrowings from many sources to fit their particular strengths and situations.

BEFORE LOOKING FURTHER AT EVANGELICALS

The advice to borrow creatively from someone else's style has important qualifiers. One is whether we can have the assurance that the Lord is actually working through such styles as ways of staying with people in today's cultures. But more important is whether we can be assured that the Gospel being expressed is the same one the borrower knows and believes.

In this time and country the Lord seems to laying very visible blessings on the ministries of Christians known collectively as Evangelicals. It is hard to avoid noting their vitality in church growth, missions, and media outreach. The churches Baumann describes are all Evangelical in one way or another. While each adds originality, all share a common denominator that in today's usage is described as Evangelical.

But is the Evangelical common denominator something Lutherans share? That identification needs clarification, and this is more than just a matter of checking terms. Conscious of their substance, Lutherans need to be sure Evangelical styles are worth looking at. Do they proclaim the same Gospel? We are all aware of the historic name "The *Evangelical* Lutheran Church." But how much does the current use of that term differ from its historical Lutheran meaning? Can faithful Lutherans accept for consideration the expressions of church life it now commonly describes?

In the last several decades the name "Evangelical" has taken on specialized meaning in American religious life. Actually it has several meanings. A leading Evangelical historian George Marsden distinguishes three. Most basic is a characteristic theology, which we will have to look at. Most apparent is use of the term to describe a broad movement among conservative Protestant churches. This is mostly a matter of style, and indeed it is this style we want to observe in some detail. The name can also be used to identify a loose collection of institutions, like colleges and mission agencies, that serve a particular constituency. In this sense it is almost like a super denomination.[1] I am not going to suggest that Lutherans consider a formal alliance with those institutions. They are too loose a collection for us to try to define over against them the kind of precise relationship Lutherans prefer. Nor is the effort necessary. The style of that movement is more important to consider.

The style is worth considering because of the theological substance described in the current meaning of the name "Evangelical." Above all else, it summarizes some basic, distinctive theological emphases. I believe conservative Lutherans are in sympathy with the most basic of those emphases. Lutheran theology need not be sacrificed to borrow from Evangelical style. When current Evangelical leaders look at American church bodies, they usually consider The Lutheran Church—Missouri Synod to be in the same theological camp they are. This is especially true after the doctrinal battles of the 1970s.

Evangelicals seldom write creeds and may differ in particulars of how they express their belief. But the pillars of their theology should be very familiar to conservative Lutherans. Marsden offers this summary of their characteristic theology. Evangelicals are Christians who emphasize:

1. the Reformation doctrine of the final authority of Scripture;
2. the real historical character of God's saving work recorded in Scripture;
3. eternal salvation only through personal trust in Christ;
4. the importance of evangelism and missions;
5. the importance of a spiritually transformed life.[2]

I am most familiar with further specifics of one representative Evangelical theology, that presented in the Statement of Faith of Fuller Theological Seminary. How that theology translates itself into a plan of action is presented in Fuller's statement of its Mission Beyond the Mission. I can fully affirm both while also affirming by subscription the Confessions of the Evangelical Lutheran Church.

If conservative Lutherans want to look beyond their denominational borders, are there better places to consider? Certainly they will continue to look at fellow Lutherans. But American Protestantism, including Lutheranism, is in the process of realigning itself. Do conservative Lutherans want to look for practical insights among churches with an operational theology that doubts the final authority of Scripture? Do they want to consider the style of churches that neglect any of the theological emphases highlighted in Marsden's summary?

It is possible to be both Lutheran and Evangelical. That can be done as part of a movement, without having to invest energy in sorting out formal institutional relationships. The style of that movement should be the focus.

CHAPTER 5

Seeing Village and Camp Differences

Current Evangelicalism is predominately an Anglo-American phenomenon. In almost all its forms it is an expression of the unique American experience of English-speaking Christians. With few exceptions, Evangelical churches left behind European church traditions almost from their beginnings. In George Marsden's explanation, American Evangelicals have all been shaped by the experience of living in a democratic society that places an emphasis on choosing for oneself and on simple populist approaches.[1]

In contrast, much of early Lutheranism in this country preferred to retain a native language other than English and to function as ethnic church bodies with their special European immigrant roots still in mind. Even in America the Lutheran experience was shaped by memories of a home church heavily influenced by state authority that controlled and limited choices.

What is at stake for many Lutherans today is whether they continue to function—consciously or unconsciously—as a separate ethnic church, trying to preserve a distinctive culture all their own. Or will they follow the mobile Lord into the future with an openness and a readiness to move beyond old ethnicity? If they want to respond more effectively to a society that stresses personal choices to a previously unimaginable degree, the Evangelical movement can give a few pointers.

VILLAGE AND CAMP ROOTS

Historic Lutheran ways and current Evangelical ways can be understood better by concentrating on their social roots. The implications can be worked out by focusing on two images. Lutheran roots are rather firmly planted in homogeneous, stable rural villages. I will call that a *village church* setting. Evangelical roots go back to a mixture of people on the move and coming together for special occasions. Theirs is a history of revivals, crusades, and camps. I suggest looking at that as a *camp church* setting.

The key difference is in assumptions about what to do with the fellowship of Christians which is basic to being church. Lutherans tend to assume that Christian community, or fellowship, already exists among those gathered in Christ's name, and ministry is oriented toward the *preservation* of it. Evangelicals tend to see individuals not yet in the community of Christians, and they orient their ministry toward the beginnings of faith and the *initiation* of fellowship with one another.

The style issue for Lutheran Christians is how much to shift their emphasis toward the initiation of fellowship in church life. In modern American society, I think it increasingly difficult to concentrate mostly on preserving church community, because its existence can no longer be taken as a simple assumption.

Village Church

What is a village church? Its roots go back to hundreds of years of long-established small towns and villages that dominated European society before this century. Each was a rather self-sufficient center for the social and economic life of families that lived in that same area for generations. For governance purposes, that center defined a geographic district called a parish. The Christian ministry carried on in that village was a parish church. Significantly, Lutherans today still call the local church a parish, and the minister is a parish pastor.

I can bring the village setting closer to current times through the example of my own family history. Both my father and mother grew up in village churches in rural Illinois. Most of their farmer neighbors were German Lutherans, and the Lutheran church was the main center of activity for their social life. I carry childhood memories of visits to relatives where it seemed as if everybody knew everything about everybody else. That was believable because they did so much of their work, shopping, recreation, *and worship* together. There was a high overlap between their everyday community and their church community.

I myself grew up in a big city. But I still experienced the remnants of a village church.

That area of the city was loaded with European ethnic groups, like Poles, Greeks, and Irish, each with their Catholic, Orthodox, Reformed, or Lutheran church. My home church, St. Matthews, had been started at the turn of the century among the German laborers in the industrial section a few blocks away. For most of its history it was a church members walked to. Thus they lived relatively close together and had plenty of opportunity to interact outside of church life. My pastor-father still preached German services into the 1960s. Many similar villagelike churches existed in other great urban centers of Missouri Synod strength, like Milwaukee, Chicago, and St. Louis.

Significantly, my home church closed its doors about 10 years ago. It suffered a lingering decline after the great migrations out to the suburbs in the 1950s. Except for a few elderly left behind, the village for all practical purposes disappeared. But its children, now adult leaders of suburban churches, carried with them a village church style.

Camp Church

In contrast, Evangelicals typically do not have a history of such identity with a fixed and stable church community. Theirs is a background of Americans restlessly on the move, ready and anxious to cut off their ties with the old country, relying on themselves to develop a new culture. Evangelical roots go back to people who found themselves newcomers in new towns with little in common except their hopes for a better future. When Lutheran, as well as Catholic, immigrants came as newcomers, they set about restoring as much as they could of what they had left behind, and they turned to their old country customs and relationships for their identity. The people who became Evangelicals made up their identity as they went along. They looked mostly to the Bible for guidance, not centuries of tradition. They could not assume a church community that already existed, even if only in memory. Preservation was not their

53

main task. They had to concentrate on initiating fellowship in the Lord.

I suggest the image of "camp" to contrast with "village." It conveys the idea of a temporary gathering of people who are likely to move on to someplace else. Indeed temporary gatherings were the formative experience for Evangelicals. These were camplike revivals, many of which turned into ongoing summer camps. Such revivals were special occasions that fostered intense religious experiences. They were a time for fresh starts in the Lord. People would come from a wide area to hear the Gospel message day after day, to renew their personal commitments as believers, and to feel their fellowship. Then they would scatter back to their routine life somewhere else.

For a camp church experience today, look to Billy Graham and his crusades. He is from a long line of great Evangelical revivalists, like Charles Finney and Dwight Moody in the 19th century. But summer church camps are also an example. Bible camps are now Lutheran enough to be the theme of the Lutheran float in the 1986 Tournament of Roses Parade in Pasadena. Think of a camp where people come from all over and are mostly strangers to each other. Faith and fellowship are expressed differently in that setting. The style is more basic and informal. The emphasis is on a special experience. Because time is short, it is an experience camp leaders try to offer quickly and directly.

Is there anything inherently wrong with a camp church? I think not. Nor is there anything inherently wrong with a village church. These are two different settings for coming together as Christians. Consider now the styles of church life that emerge from these differences.

BORN AND REBORN

The significant characteristic of a village church is that the members are born into it. That is in contrast to the camp church emphasis on being born again as the starting point.

A village church is the result of stability in community relationships. Being born into a given church is the natural first step in the pattern of growing up, living, and dying in one locality. The pattern assumes that one's parents were part of that community and in due time one's children will be, too. The church community was usually there before its current participants came along, and the church's task is to help them find their appropriate place in it. That is why village churches emphasize the baptism of infants as the God-given initiation into the community. That is why they emphasize confirmation as the time to establish a conscious, personal accountability to the community of faith. Almost everything thereafter becomes a matter of preserving what was handed on. Someone who moves away is expected to resume the pattern in the village church nearest the new place of residence, and that one should be very much like the one left behind.

As noted, Lutherans like to call the local congregation a parish, and the minister is a parish pastor. That term does not describe people. It identifies a district with defined boundaries. The assumption is that if a Christian lives within those boundaries, he or she enters the life of that village church or parish.

A camp church is the result of instability or impermanence in community relations. It happens among people on the move, who have little common history. A camp church has to start its community of faith over and over again. The unavoidable starting point is for each person to have a clear, conscious self-professed personal relationship with Christ. These Christians cannot rely on togetherness happening in the course of everyday life. What brings these believers together is the opportunity to affirm and celebrate a new and different life. That is why Evangelicals place such an emphasis on being born again in Christ. Consciousness of that life-transforming event is their only reliable basis for initiating fellowship in Christ. Stories of personal new life form the common memory. Rebirth to new life is the shared commitment that keeps this temporary church community going. Camp church may appear to be just recreation, but associate it with re-creation and it makes more sense.

Oversimplified, in a village church, belonging comes before consciously believing. That can happen through Baptism, when someone is born into an established community of faith. In a camp church, consciously believing comes before belonging. That is important when the community of faith has to establish itself each time anew.

Which is the right view? I believe Scripture allows both ways.

My point is that churches have to develop their styles of ministry in view of the social realities they face.

VILLAGE AND CAMP CHURCH SPIRITUALITY

Both a village church and a camp church look for the Holy Spirit to move among them. They look in different ways.

The Lutheran village church expects the Holy Spirit to come through God's Word and church community in very quiet, orderly, and predictable ways. These believers look to Him to touch them as they consider God's Word and respectfully participate in the sacraments. They look to Him to move them calmly to acts of reverence and to greater understanding. Lutherans want to encounter the Spirit patiently and slowly through prescribed liturgies, lessons, and authorized leaders.

It is understandable that a village church shies away from uncontrolled spontaneous experiences. The village church has to be church for everybody in that district. It cannot afford to confuse its members or to offend their faith. Theoretically those believers have no place else to go. Their church has to avoid situations that would cause members to be suspicious of each other. Impersonal control is very important, lest members put their relationships at risk. Lutheran style emphasizes the Spirit of community preservation.

Camp church spirituality looks for the Holy Spirit who works new beginnings. The Spirit still comes through God's Word, but He is expected to come quickly and decisively, right now. He comes to bring new personal confidence in God's gracious salvation in Christ. These believers look for Him to move them to fresh responses, new commitments, and immediate feelings of togetherness. Since they may well be moving on soon, they do not have to worry so much about order and control, offices and customs. They are more ready to open up their feelings for Him to move them in spontaneous ways to unexpected decisions. Camp church spirituality looks for the spirit of heightened joy and commitment to overshadow the spirit of routine reverence through familiar formalities.

Which is the right view? They both can be. The two expectations, however, do differ in the amount of risk these two types of churches are prepared to take in their response life. That attitude, I think, is shaped to a large degree by whether the emphasis is on belonging first or believing first. Because of its setting, a well-established village church can assume belonging and does not have to take many risks. But as the setting changes, new risks may be unavoidable.

THE NEW BELIEVERS AND THE CAMP CHURCH

In the previous chapter I highlighted the challenge of learning new subtleties of communicating the Gospel to American cultural subgroups that are becoming more diverse. I mentioned that these increasingly include our own children. Without anything dramatic happening to them, many find themselves part of a culture that is attracted to camp church ways of finding and expressing their faith. Ministering to them would seem to make the riskiness of camp church ways increasingly unavoidable for old churches.

How the culture shifted is described by Carl Dudley, a Presbyterian professor at McCormick Seminary. He was most concerned about the impact on older established church bodies like his. His book has another instructive title: *Where Have All Our People Gone?*[2] Dudley offers a very readable digest of the work of a number of sociological researchers who looked at what happened to the membership of such mainline churches as Episcopalian, Presbyterian, and United Church of Christ.[3] As is well known, those denominations experienced a significant loss of members. What happened? To Dudley's question we can add the observation that this loss occurred during the same period when many Evangelical churches mushroomed in size. Why is that?

Dudley centers the answer to his question of where the people went on the phenomenon of what he calls the New Believers. These are the young adults who ordinarily would have been in the older, established church bodies. They constitute the bulk of those who left, or did not continue, or did not follow former patterns of involvement. He describes these New Believers as having the significant characteristic of wanting to believe before belonging. Thus, they tend to become uncomfortable with a church life that expects them to belong before they consciously work out their personal faith. This means they have little loyalty that church leaders can take for granted.

He attributes the reason to a fundamental shift in values among the youth generation of the 1960s and 1970s. Their distrust of institutions of any kind was well recognized then, during that period of social unrest. Many were and still are Christians. But they place a new stress on some expectations that accompany a loss of old loyalties. Paramount is an emphasis on personal religious experience. For them, experience is the entry into faith. In Dudley's summary, they see their personal experience as necessary to precede believing, and believing has to occur before belonging.

The New Believers also look for a spiritual, even mystical faith, one that comes from being touched by the supernatural reality they want to believe in. A style of church life that communicates a personal flatness leaves them looking for something else. They still want community, even when they back away from loyalties to their parents' community. But it has to be the right kind—indeed, one that offers personal religious experience. Groups are expected to provide a way for each member to find personal fulfillment and continual satisfaction.

The sequence highlighted by Dudley is significant. His observation is that the New Believers expect to move first from personal religious experience to believing and then to belonging. They are able especially to separate believing from belonging. The old believers in established mainline churches are much more used to keeping the two coupled together.

Drawing from those observations, we can see a significant reason why Evangelical churches have experienced growth at a time of decline among other Christian denominations. Which churches are best prepared to reach out to the New Believers? It would be those with a style that emphasizes belonging only after consciously believing. That is camp church style. This is the style that has been formative for the Evangelicals.

With their relatively short history of revivals and their newer churches, Evangelicals have not wanted to take belonging for granted, nor have they had the circumstances to make that possible. They expect believing to come first, and they resist initiating children into the community without a conscious profession of faith. Among adults who do not know each other, believing cannot be taken for granted either. That is why Evangelicals emphasize the having and telling of personal religious experiences. That is why they so often look for the Spirit to come quickly and decisively. It is no coincidence that the growing churches have a camp church background of adeptness at helping people move along the sequence of personal experience, to believing, to belonging.

NEW SKILLS FOR POST-VILLAGE TIMES

The village church pattern is based on the opposite sequence. The question is what to do about that, if anything.

In the village pattern a member typically is born into the parish church. Thus belonging comes first. The faith instilled by Baptism is something infants can have, and the community that accepts this new member also accepts the responsibility for nurturing his or her faith, specifically through sponsors. After careful nurture the maturing child is led to a personal profession of faith, celebrated as confirmation by the community to which he or she already belongs. Everyone hopes that, in the course of church life over the years, faith may be deepened and enriched through peak personal experiences, but these are not necessary to the pattern. A traditional village church is typically more adept at celebrating corporate encounters with God than at highlighting the deeply personal religious experiences of its individual members.

There are many good reasons for this pattern. They are deeply imbedded in centuries of pastoral familiarity with the fragility of personal experience as a basis for saving faith. William Hordern reviews the significance of Luther's theology for understanding today's experiential religion, which he regards as the dominant theme in North American religion since the early 1970s. He recalls two reasons for Luther's emphasis on the outward work of the Holy Spirit in Word and sacraments. One is that inner experiences are not dependable, since they come and go and differ in strength and intensity. Only the outward promises of Word and sacraments can give firm assurance. Second, if inner experiences become primary, believers may soon begin to trust in themselves and turn away from Christ.[4]

The parish pattern has many strengths. At its best it can support a rich church life that is a source of continued nurture and necessary stability for believers as they go through the various phases of their personal and religious lives. The pattern is typically at its best in an established village setting, either rural or urban. A well-functioning village church is a long-standing, real community. Its members are known and cared for. Active participants can be sure of who they are and where they belong. A parish church can be a wonderful place for developing personal confidence to risk exciting growth in Christ.

But for all its strengths, the parish church has inherent weaknesses. One set of weaknesses is very familiar to parish pastors, who continuously work at developing skills for overcoming them. I think another set is only recently becoming apparent, and overcoming these weaknesses calls for new skills among church leaders.

The familiar weaknesses can be summarized in the term "parochial." This has come to imply a narrowness of thought, interests, or activity. Village church members often seem overly content with what they have. As many pastors see it, that is too often a rather elementary understanding of Christian faith and life. Also, mission and outreach frequently remain of minimal concern.

Camp is not the only alternative to village. As a corrective for the parochialism of a village church, many pastors have focused on the image of the university as a source of insights that will improve their ministry skills. Put pejoratively, village church life can seem unsophisticated and self-serving. One style of ministry popular in recent decades would aim at raising the level of sophistication and expanding the horizons of the church life, paralleling the educational work of universities. Indeed, as the proportion of American adults with a college-level education increased dramatically after World War II, members themselves expected their church life to become more sophisticated and broad-minded. The liturgical movement is a reflection of a more cultured and aesthetic style of worship. Concentration on major social issues also becomes a much more important form of ministry.

Despite such efforts to grow out of a village perspective, however, Lutheran styles of ministry have not moved far beyond a village mentality in one important respect. The style is prone to assume that the old patterns of village parish life are still intact. Therein lies a different set of weaknesses that are now emerging. The parish pattern is based on long-term stability of relationships among members, such as villagers would have, especially when they share an ethnic background. Churches that have benefited from the strength of well-established loyalties have an especially difficult adjustment to its absence.

Can church loyalty be taken for granted today? The answer to that question is pivotal for exploring styles of ministry.

In some parts of the country the rural and urban villages with their church life may still be functioning as of old. But there are strong social forces pulling community life apart, and they affect church life as well. Impermanence and instability in economic and social relationships are becoming characteristic of American society today. We are seeing the aftereffects of decades of high mobility and loosened loyalties to old institutions in general. Family life has undergone dramatic change, especially with the rise of the divorce rate. Fewer people seem to place a high value on long-term commitments. Sociologists have little trouble describing the instability that seems much more prevalent today. The New Believers are one of the consequences.

Dudley's insights on the New Believers confirm the hazards of relying on a ministry style that assumes a preexisting church community among participants. The loosened loyalties that come from social instability and shifting cultural values have to have implications for ministry. Most directly, they translate into the need for improved skills to initiate a church community of believers and to build, rebuild, and rebuild it again. Post-village skills call for increased pastoral ability to minister among people who come as strangers, do not expect to stay long, and measure their provisional participation according to the experiences it gives them. Such skills will come from learning new ways of experiencing the Gospel and organizing church life in a context of few loyalties that can be taken for granted.

Lasting, sure fellowship with God is the substance of Lutheranism. That should be just the antidote for ministering to a transient society. God's promise of His reliable presence, conveyed through Word and sacraments and expressed by His church, can be an anchor to people whose lives are filled with uncertainty. Yet traditional Lutheran style today often gets in the way of helping others find that presence if they do not already belong. The ministry skills of that style seem more honed for the preservation of faith among those who have it than for beginning it among strangers.

The camp style of Evangelicals emphasizes skills to facilitate personal religious experiences as avenues to belief and belonging. Lutheranism will always regard that as risky. But post-village skills for Lutherans will have to focus on personal experiences in some way. The challenge is to learn how to do that better while keeping all the strengths of Word and sacrament ministry.

CHAPTER 6

Some Evangelism and Marketing Questions

Old churches accepting Jesus' challenge to "Come and see" can go as tourists or as seekers. Tourists see new sights but head home with random observations that usually do not change how they live. Seekers look for answers. They are ready for something new and better. But seekers need to be critical, lest they find answers that are wrong for their home situation, and it is important for old-church seekers to return home.

Some churches do not encourage church sightseeing even as tourists. Part 1 addressed reservations of that sort. God has a history of blessing such exploration by using it to stir up new life in old churches.

Lutherans have special encouragement and resources for looking at other churches. It so happens that two of the best books available for describing denominational differences are by Lutheran scholars. These are F. E. Mayer's *The Religious Bodies of America,*[1] and A. C. Piepkorn's *Profiles in Belief.*[2] These two works are significant church-supported investments in taking other churches seriously. They say something about the thoroughness of Lutheran dedication to church life.

Such resources are written tour guides. They can be very helpful to tourists. They are basic for seekers, too. But seekers ask their questions differently. Their looking shares the tourist's curiosity, but they are ready to learn something that can change what they are doing.

The seeking I advocate is selective. Old churches whose evangelism has become difficult have something to learn from growing churches. Looking there, the seeker's basic question is "What?" What is going on that can help explain their growth, and what can that mean for a church which is not growing? Seekers will do well to select matters of style to look at. Thus, the seeker will also ask "How?" How is the Gospel presented in that growing church and how can a home church do its Gospel work differently?

Those practical questions lead back to substantive matters of beliefs. I am not advocating that churches question the Why of their theology. Indeed, exploration of other churches can be a fine time to reaffirm a church's substance. Assessing styles is the task highlighted here. That is primarily a matter of Whats and Hows. I will explore these four style-assessment questions:

1. What are these people seeking when they come?
2. How is Christ held up for them?
3. How do they wait upon the Holy Spirit?
4. What is the combination that makes this church spirit infectious?

The second and third questions are the center of evangelism. They focus on God in action and on church-style interpretation of that action. Scripture remains the necessary source for evaluating any conclusions to be drawn. We will have to check all answers against that source.

The first question looks at the context for evangelism. It focuses on expectations people bring to their encounter with a church. The last is a summary of the style that affects outreach. Both force attention to the human side of the evangelism equation, with Christ and the Holy Spirit on the other side. The human enterprise of marketing can help define the perceptions of the people to be reached. I will draw on some insights from marketing.

The next chapter suggests some answers to be found in various types of Evangelical churches.

WAITING UPON THE HOLY SPIRIT

In Luke's account of our Lord's ascension, Jesus left us with only one directive: "Stay in the city until you have been clothed with power from on high" (Luke 24:49). His previous words were promise and prediction. The prediction was that repentance and forgiveness of sins would be preached in His name to all nations. The promise was that Jesus would send them what also His Father promised—"power from on high."

Even though the question of how a church waits upon the Holy Spirit is third in my outline for assessing what seekers are to look for, it is basic to understanding the others. The "power from on high" is the Holy Spirit, who in Christian confession "proceeds from the Father and the Son" (Athanasian Creed). It is the Holy Spirit who is God at work when people come to faith and grow in love.

How do disciples wait upon the Spirit? What should they look for? How do they expect the Spirit to come, and what do they want Him to do? There are different answers to these questions. What we as believers do sometimes gets us more directly in the path of the Spirit's movement. Other things we do seem to hinder the Spirit's work, to resist what He is trying to do in us. "Spirituality" is a word that describes the way we shape our experience of the Holy Spirit. A church can have a distinctive spirituality. To look at styles of evangelism, these styles of spirituality have to be recognized. How growing churches shape their experience of the Holy Spirit helps explain their infectious human spirit.

Birth from Above

The objective for evangelism is that people "Come and see" Jesus' saving presence for them. Jesus gave us a clear lesson on how that happens. It is in a discourse that leads up to the much-loved Gospel text, John 3:16: "For God so loved the world that he gave his one and only Son, that whoever believes in him shall not perish but have eternal life." How does such belief begin?

Nicodemus wanted to know. He is the man Jesus was talking to. God was present in Jesus Christ right before his eyes, but Nicodemus was not sure he could see Him. His plight describes so many people today in a supposedly Christianized American society. Most have heard the necessary information. But faith is more than hearing or seeing a description of God in Christ.

Jesus' answer to Nicodemus was that to see God's saving presence, you have to be born again: "No one can see the kingdom of God unless he is born again" (John 3:3). Actually, "born again" can also mean "born from above." This is a more literal translation. It is clear from Jesus' expanded explanation in verse 5 that this means being born of the Spirit.

To be "born" also says a little more in the Greek verb than is usually recognized. Birth is not so much a point in time. It is a passing on of life from one person to another. The verb is the same Matthew uses to tell that "Abraham begat Isaac" (KJV), followed by all the other "begats" in his first chapter. Jesus was explaining that the Spirit from above has to pass on new life, spiritual life, to us. Then we will recognize God's presence in Christ. To be "born again" is to come under the influence of the Holy Spirit.

"Born again" is of course the hallmark description of modern Evangelicals. They want to be known as born again Christians. Lutherans get uncomfortable with that insignia of faith. When asked on a questionnaire whether they are born again Christians, they are likely to hesitate and qualify their yes. Evangelicals seem eager to tell when and how they were born again. For most Lutherans, their rebirth happened in Baptism as infants, and they want to make clear that they do not have any dramatic stories to tell.

The initiation of faith through infant baptism will never be just a matter of style for Lutherans. But language is. There is no reason to be defensive over against born again language. Believing Lutherans have had new life passed on to them through the Holy Spirit. Without qualification, they, too, are born again Christians.

When they use the phrase, the real issue for Evangelicals is whether a person's current life is under the influence of the Spirit, however that may have started. They want to witness that in Christ they recognize God's presence in their lives. Evangelical church style is oriented toward helping people begin and continue to recognize that presence as directly as possible. It is a presence granted by God's grace. *Sola gratia* is as pivotal for Evangelicals as it is for Lutherans, even though they may not talk about it in carefully defined classical vocabulary. In a style with little memory of debates over the centuries, they prefer to talk about what God in His grace is doing in their lives right now.

Lutherans should have no problem wanting to talk about the same thing. But sometimes their style gets in the way. I think that is partly because of village church ways of looking for the Holy Spirit.

Open to the Spirit

As I noted in the previous chapter, village church spirituality looks for the Holy Spirit to come in calm, orderly, and predictable ways. I think Jesus was very clear that the Spirit comes in other ways as well. Look at what He tells Nicodemus to expect: "You should not be surprised at my saying, 'You must be born again [or born from on high].' The wind blows wherever it pleases. You hear its sound, but you cannot tell where it comes from or where it is going. So it is with everyone born of the Spirit" (John 3:7–8). It is as if Jesus is telling us to expect the unexpected.

How well does a church's style enable believers to cope with a Holy Spirit of whom it cannot be predicted where He is coming from or where He is going? A village church tries very hard to reduce the unexpected in their midst. The understandable reasons were identified earlier. These revolve around the emphasis on preservation and stability. But a camp church does not have to be so cautious. In fact, it thrives on the unexpected. People come looking for fresh responses and new commitments. They expect the Holy Spirit to move them in spontaneous ways to decisions they do not anticipate.

In a village church the presence of the Holy Spirit can indeed be noticed, but the style often makes Him hard to recognize. Participants in a camp church often find they can recognize Him more readily.

What makes Lutherans nervous about the free and unfettered Spirit is the worry that it may be the wrong spirit. The one they are ready to recognize always works through God's Word. Without Scripture, God's followers cannot be sure of where He is in relation to them. One of the strengths of a village church is the customs and formalities it has for testing the Spirit with the well-considered Word. But sometimes it is just those formalities that hinder the Spirit. To test the unexpected Spirit, a camp church has to rely directly on the Word itself, because it does not have many traditions.

Worries about the spirituality of a camp church can be addressed by asking whether Scripture is kept front and center in what is happening. It is hard to go far wrong then. I think that is the meaning of the Lutheran emphasis on *sola scriptura*. God's promise is that His Spirit will be where His Word is preached.

Lutherans who are fully determined to remain Bible-based in their proclamation have to assess other churches according to whether they share that intent. It is apparent that Evangelicals do. There is not much question that they today have an enviable reputation for taking God's written Word in Scripture very seriously. That in itself is a good reason for looking at the way they try to communicate it.

HOLDING UP CHRIST

The second assessment question asks how Christ is held up within a church. It inquires about the style of presenting Christ as Savior. What dimensions of His past and current presence are featured? How is His redeeming work presented?

The phrase "holding up Christ" comes from Jesus' explanation to Nicodemus. Towards the end of the dialog, He said: "As Moses lifted up the snake in the desert, so the Son of Man must be lifted up, that everyone who believes in him may have eternal life" (John 3:14–15). Here is where Jesus lays out what His followers can take upon themselves to do. For God the Holy Spirit we have to wait, but God the Son we can lift up for others to see. That is work we can choose to do, and we can choose how to do it. We can also learn how to do it better. How well we do our job is to be seen in how successfully the Holy Spirit can move to faith those to whom we try to show this Christ.

The reference to Moses and the serpent is from the story in Numbers 21. The people had lost sight of God's presence in their midst. All they could see was monotonous food, thirst, and death. Then God added to their woes the punishment of serpents to bite them and cause more death. Finally they were ready to repent and turn again to the Lord. Here was the good news God delivered through a job given to Moses: "The Lord said to Moses, 'Make a snake and put it up on a pole; anyone who is bitten can look at it and live' " (Num. 21:8).

In evangelism the job is to hold up Christ, so that all who are bitten today, when they see Him, shall live. In some respects that job is easy. We just have to make Jesus Christ visible. But in other respects it is quite difficult. People have to see Him. The verb really means they have to recognize Him. They have to recognize that in

68

Him they are offered a new life, a life without end. When Nicodemus recognized that Jesus was God standing before him, then the Holy Spirit could work on moving him to faith.

The Village Church Handicap

I offer a very loaded generalization at this point. Village church Lutherans have an inherent limitation in evangelism. They bring a handicap to the task of holding up Christ in ways many people of today can recognize. It is not that Lutherans follow an outmoded Christ. Rather it is that most have never known a life without Him. Most were carefully nurtured from earliest childhood to look to Him as the source of God's saving presence in their lives. Thus it is difficult to feel what others are looking for when they do not already know Jesus as their Savior. Words and acts that mean a lot to lifelong church members do not always convey the same meaning to those without that background. Because of their distinct culture, Lutherans, as well as many other old-church believers, are prone to raise up Christ in ways that do not get the attention of people different from them.

That generalization does not call for an apology from Lutheran Christians. How they nurture their children is a great strength of this church. I use the generalization to point to the challenge in evangelizing adults outside the existing historic community, as well as the children with loosened loyalties to that community. It is the challenge to master new subtleties of style for communicating the Gospel to people with different life experiences. The more different they are, the more old-church witnessing has to adjust to be heard in their dialect.

ADDRESSING FELT NEEDS

The necessary first question in evangelism is: What are these people seeking when they come? This assesses the context for a church's life and style, that is, the people who are being reached. What needs do they feel and what are they looking for.

The summary last question for evangelism is: What is the combination that makes this church spirit (with a small s) infectious? This is a question to be asked of growing churches that indeed have a distinctive *esprit* and a spreading impact. The same question can be rephrased for churches that are not growing: What interferes with the spread of this church's spirit? Either way, the question helps to summarize the style of evangelism to be assessed.

I can rephrase this last question yet another way. It is with a style of language that neither Evangelicals nor Lutherans use and that is harsh to churchly dialect. But it is a language that is very common in our current culture. For years I taught management in several business schools. I cannot help but look at evangelism as a marketing task. Using that vocabulary, what is the packaging that delivers a church's substantive product most effectively? The answer comes by figuring out the first question: What are the consumers looking for; what are their felt needs? Market research helps identify those needs. I will drop the marketing vocabulary after drawing some insights from the discipline.

Contrary to popular opinion, marketing is not just promotion and selling. It is foremost a matter of understanding what potential consumers want when they are shopping to fill their needs. Good marketers rely heavily on market research. Using their consumer insights, they help shape and package the product offering so that it has a better chance of getting attention and acceptance.

Engineering and Marketing

When a company brings a product to the marketplace, it usually relies on engineers to design the offering, so that it delivers what is promised. Engineers are technical experts. If given a chance, they will usually try to design the best product possible. Unfortunately engineers do not always understand consumers well. The business world is full of examples of excellently designed product offerings that did not find many buyers. One way or another, such products turn out to be something too few consumers are looking for.

Companies that want their product well accepted learn to listen to the potential buyers. When they are serious about adjusting to consumer wants, they become a marketing-oriented enterprise. A company that prefers to listen mostly to the technical experts remains an engineering-oriented firm. In today's complicated marketplace there are few engineering-oriented businesses that are consistently successful without acquiring the marketing expertise of listening to their customers. Companies that offer a product of lasting worth have to rely on their engineers. But they do better when they insist that the engineers learn to shape and package the product according to changing consumer expectations. They add marketing expertise to their technical expertise.

The automobile industry provides an example. Volkswagen sales expanded rapidly in the 1950s and 1960s. The "bug" was a product that met a need, and it was designed with respected German engineering. But sales in this country declined significantly in the 1970s. Consumer needs and style preferences changed. Engineering oriented, Volkswagen executives were slow to react and relied too long on this single "well designed" package. Because of its early sales success, the company had not developed strong marketing expertise. Growth returned when they paid attention to market diversity and learned how to design their offering in a variety of packages, from the Rabbit to the Audi. They learned how to better balance technical and marketing expertise.

A comparison between automobiles and churches would be crass. But assessing a church's "engineering" orientation or "marketing" orientation is not inappropriate. I hope I have explained the term well enough so that "marketing" does not carry heavy negative connotations. How does a church design the way it lifts up Christ for others to see? Does it look mostly to technical expertise in theology and church history, or does it rely more on its understanding of the felt needs of the people it is trying to reach?

Striving for a Balance

There does not have to be a forced choice between either engineering or marketing, between technical expertise or consumer expectations. The best is both/and. Each in its own way, churches can strive for such a balance. Churches that sustain infectious growth have usually found such a combination.

Historically, Lutherans have been engineering-oriented. They typically design their offering with solid technical expertise in theology, backed up by centuries of the packaging experience that tradition provides. Because of their history as an established church among believers with few options, I think they are weak on marketing, that is, marketing understood as listening to the needs and expectations of other people, who do have choices. More precisely, I think Lutherans shape and package their Gospel offering according to the felt needs of only a small segment of American society. That "market" is now getting smaller. But there are millions more people who are looking for God's presence in their lives. Can Lutherans learn how to package their offering better? Can they find better ways to hold up Christ so that others can recognize Him as the source of new life for them, too?

Growth trends make it evident where the marketing strength is in American Christianity today. A number of Evangelical churches seem to have a flair for it. They seem able to package the Gospel in ways that meet the felt needs of increasing numbers of Americans. How do they do it? That is the subject of the next chapter.

Lutherans will undoubtedly have technical engineering reservations about the quality and durability of those offerings. Through interaction with Evangelical churches they may be able to suggest to them improvements in their various designs. Meanwhile, through an assessment of Evangelical styles, Lutherans can gain insights for improving their own designs. Such exploration can be regarded as a form of market research.

CHAPTER 7

Assessing Evangelical Styles

Church seekers can go and look at other churches by reading books. Otherwise this book would serve no purpose. But reading is best done as preparation for personally going and physically seeing and hearing. That is how style becomes most apparent.

During my several years among Evangelicals, I have seen and heard. My seminary observations were supplemented with visits to a number of growing Evangelical congregations. These happen to be in Southern California, a fact that unavoidably introduces a regional bias into these observations. But then, this region often serves as a forerunner of trends that move across the country.

The church-assessment questions outlined in the previous chapter emerged in the course of my observations. In evolving forms, they were my attempt to make sense out of what I saw. I was looking at the practical level of the dynamics at work that seemed to make the human spirit of a particular church infectious. What I was trying to understand can be called popular religion, or folk religion. Years of experience doing case analyscs in management classes helped keep me attuned to the marketing implications of what I saw. At the same time, my training as a Lutheran minister helped keep theological issues in the forefront.

Among Evangelicals I can distinguish several different combinations of ingredients of dedicated Christian discipleship and church life. All share the distinctive characteristic of a high commitment to the authority of Scripture for belief and practice. But Evangelicals have different emphases in how they share God's presence, as it is conveyed through His Word. In order to aid perception and discussion, I will give names to these emphases or orientations.

To use the marketing vernacular of the last chapter one last time, these are the "packaging" of a church's offering.

Typologies are hazardous and inevitably oversimplified. The effort is worthwhile only to the extent that it aids perception of differences that otherwise might not be apparent and then increases understanding of their possible implications. This attempt is intended to help old churches, particularly Lutheran ones, become more confident in considering and choosing among Evangelical styles they might adapt to their own existing style.

I gained confidence in the typology of Evangelicals when I discovered one offered by an observer more experienced than I. Samuel S. Hill Jr. is a professor of religion who brings an "insider's" view from his lifelong Baptist experience. He acknowledges a bit of distance marked by his confirmation into the Episcopal Church several years before writing "The Shape and Shapes of Popular Southern Piety."[1] His terminology will be noted.

I suggest these descriptive categories for distinguishing differences in style that can be seen among Evangelicals:

1. Life-plan emphasis;
2. Contact emphasis;
3. Conversion emphasis;
4. Distinctive blends.

TWO BASIC STRAINS

In Biblical usage, to believe can place the stress on being convinced or on having trust. One emphasizes faith as "being convinced that [God] exists and that his revelations or disclosures are true"; the other "lays special emphasis on trust in his power and his nearness to help."[2] These shades of difference can be seen in Evangelical churches today that offer a "life plan" emphasis or a "contact" emphasis.

Life-Plan Orientation

This is most evident in Fundamentalist churches. The preacher and church most visibly representing this style today is Jerry Falwell at Thomas Road Baptist Church in Lynchburg, Va. Charles Swindoll at First Evangelical Free Church in Fullerton, Calif., to a great extent ministers out of this style as well. Grace Community Church in the San Fernando Valley of Los Angeles is another very effective representation of a Fundamentalist style. Separate but somewhat related strains are evident among the rapidly growing Seventh-Day Adventists and Jehovah's Witnesses.

Characteristic of this orientation is an emphasis on the Word as showing God's will and plan for all people and for each person in particular. All Evangelicals, including evangelical Lutherans, take the will of God very seriously, as revealed in Christ and Scripture. Some churches are intent on interpreting that will in very specific terms for life's situations today. They want to leave little doubt about the right answers to most questions people have about what God wants them to believe and do.

Samuel Hill calls such churches "truth-oriented Evangelical Protestants (EP)," who are referred to as Fundamentalists. They teach absolute truth and require from their members solid subscription to truths as taught. As Hill notes, this is a rationalist approach that sees revealed truth as propositions, laws, and facts which are to be given assent. Their goal is "to build true, pure, 'correct' Christianity and to expose and undermine false teaching and corrupt churches and opinions."[3]

In terms of the church-assessment questions:

1. What are these people seeking when they come to these churches? A key word is certainty—certainty of who they are and what God expects of them.

2. How is Christ held up? Jesus is the Teacher of truth. He is the Source of authoritative knowledge, which is typically presented in long didactic sermons. A favorite theme is God's plan for your life.

3. How do they wait upon the Holy Spirit? Leaders in these churches expect the Holy Spirit to come through Biblically informed understanding and to move the hearers to correct, God-pleasing obedience. They look to the Spirit to bring belief as conviction of God-given truth.

4. What is the combination that makes this church spirit infectious? These are people who by the grace of God have a divine plan for life. Through God's Word in Christ they can be sure of where they are going. This is primarily content evangelism, to use the distinctions offered in the Introduction to Part 2. It becomes infec-

tious as participants share their church-related personal convictions and explain to others God's plan for their lives.

Contact Orientation

This emphasis is difficult to label. An etymologically correct term might be enthusiasm, meaning "in God." As a 19th-century movement it was called Holiness. An 18th-century version among Lutherans was called Pietism. In the 20th century there are several strains that have added new expressions. A flat, neutral term would be to call it an experiential style. I will focus on its emphasis on contact with God.

The experiential style is evident in churches that emphasize the presence of God that changes lives and brings new feelings and experiences to individuals. All Evangelicals, including evangelical Lutherans, take God's life-transforming work very seriously; by grace through Christ He gives believers new emotions of love and trust. Some churches stress these emotions in rather evident forms of joy or closeness or release of tension. They want people to experience as directly as possible the presence of God in their lives.

This style is most evident in Pentecostal churches today. Speaking in tongues is but one expression, and most of these churches follow St. Paul's admonition to discourage its appearance in corporate worship. Close cousins are various charismatic churches. The charisma are shared as gifts of God to be celebrated.

A Four Square Gospel Pentecostal church in Southern California that in recent years has had growth measured in the thousands is Church on the Way in Van Nuys, with Jack Hayford as pastor. He does not have an organized evangelism program to point to; the growth just happens, he says.[4] The Vineyard in Anaheim, Calif., pastored by John Wimber, would prefer to be considered charismatic, with an emphasis on healing. Its infectiousness is evident in the 140 congregations it has spawned throughout the country in the last 10 years.

Hill distinguishes this style as "spiritually oriented EP." He assesses this as devotional religion dwelling on and living by the Lord's intimate and constant presence. For them, "the goal of Christianity ... is to experience Him for the sake of knowing that He and His joy are what life is all about, and so to share this contagion with those who are missing out on the essence of Christianity, and, indeed, the true purpose and meaning of life." He finds this style in old-fashioned Methodism, mainline black Protestant churches, and in a more extreme form in charismatic and Pentecostal believers.[5]

To ask the church-assessment questions:

1. What are these people seeking when they come to these churches? The basic felt need is for the opportunity to feel the presence of God and to share these feelings with others.

2. How is Christ held up? Jesus is the Giver of new life, the Performer of miracles. He is offered as ready to enter a person's heart and be the Source of power for new, God-pleasing living.

3. How do they wait upon the Holy Spirit? Leaders rely on the Holy Spirit to come through the hearing of God's promises, as they are conveyed through Scripture and witnessed to by believers who have experienced His power. When the Holy Spirit comes, He is expected to give understanding but especially to touch emotions of joy and love. They look to the Spirit to bring faith as confidence of God's life-giving presence.

4. What is the combination that makes this church spirit infectious? Common descriptions are warmth and enthusiasm. These are people who, by God's grace, have experienced renewal in their feelings and relationships.

If the word "contact" is taken in its root sense of touching or feeling something, this style can be summarized as a contact orientation, offering contact with God, with one's emotions, and with fellow believers.

As noted, this contact orientation has distinct American roots in the Holiness movement of the late 19th century. In his history of the shaping of 20th-century Evangelicalism up to 1925, George Marsden shows how that movement converged with millennialism, or dispensationalism. This scheme for anticipating the future offered an intellectual framework for revivalist efforts, a framework that became closely associated with Fundamentalism. The Holiness movement propelled numerous renewal efforts of consecrated, practical Christian living and service through profound personal experience. Marsden traces the complex interaction between leaders of what became a coalition.[6] Seen in the light of the present discussion, they borrowed freely from each other. Their "camp church" setting facilitated such cross-fertilization.

The result is that Evangelicalism today is a blend of many styles. The two just assessed have carried forward these separate roots most clearly, although local churches are likely to have their own distinctive combination, usually forged by individualistic, strong-willed leaders.

Decision Orientation

One other ingredient was in the blend that shaped Evangelical style. Where dominant, it can be distinguished today as a third significant Evangelical orientation. This is an overriding emphasis on practical evangelism as winning souls for Christ. The style avoids controvesy and extreme expressions; it concentrates on the conversion of those who are lost.

Decision orientation is a good name for this style. Its distinctive flavor goes back to Dwight Moody, the dominant late-19th-century influence in American Evangelicalism. Unlike his predecessors, who were educators, Moody was by background a businessman, and he pragmatically concentrated on the single goal of preaching the Gospel to convert sinners. Another practical businessman/revivalist was Charles E. Fuller, whose radio evangelism made the style nationally known. Billy Graham epitomizes this orientation today, and he is known by many as Mr. Evangelical. His message is simple and basic, yet told in a way that engages the attention of millions a year. The style is focused on putting salvation within reach of those who can be moved to make a decision for Christ. The decision orientation is distinctly modern American. Graham keeps his approach centered on it by featuring the term in his "Hour of Decision" broadcast and *Decision* magazine.

Hill distinguishes this combination as "conversion-oriented EP." He assesses this emphasis as seeing the essence of Christianity in the seeking and finding of personal salvation. This approach "gives enormous energies to evangelism, that is, to making individuals aware of their eternally lost condition before God and to acquainting them with the pardon of sin available through accepting Christ as Savior. Their goal is to bring about every individual's new status before God in the experience of conversion."[7]

There is an inherent tension between this approach to evangelism and the sustained building up of churches. Churches are made up of those who are already converted, and with this approach the life together of those who are found often becomes incidental to the emphasis on reaching out to the lost. Old churches in particular feel this tension with what is the epitome of camp church style. Even within Evangelicalism, adapting the conversion orientation to church life is difficult. Hill points to the Southern Baptists as a conspicuous example of a blend where this emphasis has remained dominant. It is not coincidental that Billy Graham comes from Southern Baptist roots. I will comment on this particular blend shortly.

Applying the assessment questions:

1. What are these people seeking when they come to a conversion-oriented event, be it in a church or some other setting? Those who are genuinely unconverted are coming to be found and to find answers to confusion, spiritual emptiness, or loneliness. Realistically, most of those present are already consciously Christian. They come partially to see others converted and thereby to fulfill their own sense of mission. Their dominant felt need is undoubtedly to review their own decision and its meaning for their lives.

2. How is Christ held up? Jesus is the Redeemer. He is offered as the Deliverer from sin in all its many human forms, which are described with current examples.

3. How do they wait upon the Holy Spirit? The way is prepared by preaching the basic Biblical message of sin and salvation in Christ. The Holy Spirit is waited for most specifically in the time set aside for a personal decision by those present. He is expected to "turn" the individual, to work conversion and recommitment to a new life in Christ.

4. What is the combination that makes this church spirit infectious? This emphasis offers individuals the opportunity to find personal peace with God through a conscious, decisive surrender to His saving presence.

But this last question cannot be applied very well. As noted, this orientation is not primarily an expression of church but more an activity of individual evangelists on their own. Nor is infectiousness a good term to describe the dynamics. This is confrontation evangelism, where the Gospel message is conveyed not so much in a context of ongoing relationships as by a point-in-time call to a solitary personal decision for a one-on-one relationship with God. This style is clearly effective, but it is characteristically a pre-church and pre-infectious orientation.

DISTINCTIVE BLENDS

Several other blends are distinctive. One is interesting to look at but somewhat difficult for many churches to borrow from. Another provides more of a model for adaptations that denominationally affiliated old churches can make.

Southern Baptist Blend

The downward trend in church membership for mainline church bodies first became noticeable in the numbers about 1965. Since that year churches in the Southern Baptist Convention increased membership about 40%, to become by far the largest single Protestant denomination in America, larger even than any total of church bodies that share a common denominational history. In 1940 Southern Baptist and Lutheran bodies were almost equal in size (Southern Baptist, 4,949,000; Lutheran, 4,640,000). In 1985 the Southern Baptists reported membership of 14,477,000, compared to 8,274,000 for those Lutheran bodies. Clearly there are different dynamics of church growth at work.[8]

As a denomination, Southern Baptists are too large and varied to characterize with a single orientation. What is interesting is how all three of the just-described orientations are blended together, with two other ingredients that few other churches can have. Hill has listed Southern Baptists as his best example of conversion-oriented Evangelical Protestants, and he sees evangelism as their animating force. Growth is deliberate. Their outreach, of course, is largely in the South, which puts them within a region that has always maintained a distinctive culture that today remains unusually predisposed to Evangelical expressions of faith.

As observers frequently note, religion has been formative for the popular culture of the South, often described as the Bible Belt. Through revivals and "old-fashioned" southern Methodism, Holiness emphases and warm personal experiences have been a dominant strain. At the same time, the strain of Fundamentalist thought patterns has almost been taken for granted without a need to be critically defended. In Hill's assessment of Southern culture, "Observers since Frederick Law Olmsted in the 1850's down to Jimmy Carter watchers have been struck by the powerful hold on the people of the region exercised by a Christian metaphysic and notion of the providential ordering of events, but most of all, the conviction that God is very near each person to give and to require."[9]

A fourth part of the blend can be seen in the village/camp distinction. Until recent decades the South remained mostly a village society, long after the North was urbanized. More so than any other region, it still is today. The primary strengths of a village are stability and an extensive overlap between social and church community. In this context the fellowship life of a church almost takes care of itself, and church loyalties remain strong. This firm base permits an emphasis on converting the lost without overlooking the found, thus facilitating the blending of a style that is otherwise difficult to adapt to church life. Add a fifth part to the blend and Southern Baptist growth becomes even more understandable. In demographics the Sunbelt has recently had the most population growth of any part of the country.

If the village setting is where Lutherans functioned most effectively, might Southern Baptist churches be an especially good place for them to look for new styles? Not necessarily. The point of Chapter 5 is that those characteristic Lutheran settings were ethnic villages, which through assimilation are now disappearing, and that Lutherans need to learn new skills for post-village times. Lutheranism has been predominantly a Northern phenomenon and is not at home in the village culture that remains in the South.

Mainline Adaptations

A more fruitful place for Lutherans to look is distinctive blends that have emerged in other old churches. Evangelical theological and style emphases can be found in congregations that maintain their mainline denominational identity.

Many such churches have remained staunchly conservative and have gone in the direction shared by "truth-oriented" Evangelicals. However, in the last half century Presbyterian and Reformed churches with Fundamentalist agendas have typically broken off from their larger colleague denominations.

The direction of "spiritually oriented" Evangelicals has been the more frequent adaptation for those who remained in their denomination. Robert Schuller at Garden Grove Community Church near Anaheim is an interesting example. He has been steadily reasserting his identity with the Reformed Church of America. His adaptation is highly original, and he forthrightly acknowledges that he borrowed heavily from the style of Norman Vincent Peale. While Peale ministered most of his years in the RCA, he in turn directly traces his formative roots to turn-of-the-century Methodism, which was still in its revivalist Holiness phase.[10] Schuller's themes of possibility thinking, power ("Hour of Power"), hope ("Tower of Hope"), and happy, successful living are very modern expressions of contact orientation.

Among Presbyterians a number of pastors and congregations have remained firmly Evangelical in theology and have added distinctly contemporary emphases on relational outreach coupled with personal spiritual growth. Lloyd Ogilvie at the First Presbyterian Church of Hollywood is perhaps the most visible example; his featured broadcast theme is "Let God Love You."

Two sources of style change can be traced in some of these old-line denominational churches. One is the Faith at Work movement of the 1960s, which emphasized faith-based personal discovery and renewed relationships, usually through small-group encounters. Some leaders associated with that movement are Bruce Larson and Lyman Coleman. The other source is the charismatic movement of recent decades. One knowledgeable observer of Presbyterianism offers the opinion that of the large Presbyterian congregations that are growing, probably three quarters have pastors and members who affirm charismatic expressions.[11] The more dramatic forms of that style usually remain in the background of their church life.

Similar Evangelical style adaptations certainly exist in other long-established old-church denominations, especially Episcopalian. Discovering the varieties calls for more efforts to go and look.

CHAPTER 8

Touchpoints for Lutheran Adaptations

The purpose of discussing Evangelical styles is to improve our focus on what churches with other traditions might consider. Simply imitating a nearby growing church is clumsy innovation. Indeed, indiscriminate borrowing is not possible for churches that value their particular substance and unique heritage of style.

Where among Evangelicals can Lutherans most fruitfully look for style insights that can be integrated into their church life with faithfulness to Lutheran identity? The previous chapter ended with a few examples of local churches in other mainline denominations that are working toward Evangelical emphases that become distinctive blends with their own heritage. What might a Lutheran blend look like?

Three basic strains of Evangelical style have been highlighted: life-plan orientation, contact orientation, and decision orientation. The suggestion here is that exploration of contact-oriented Evangelical practices has the most potential for productive insights Lutherans can consider. The chapter heading featuring "touchpoints" for Lutheran adaptation carries that implication.

The emphasis on decision and conversion has much to offer and can certainly help improve evangelism techniques for any church. Lutherans often express caution because of a worry that the call for a decision to accept Christ will detract from the necessary understanding that an individual's justifying faith is ultimately an act of God, by grace, and not something a person can come to on his or her own. But that need not be a major reservation, for decision-oriented practitioners of evangelism are usually quite clear on *sola gratia* as they look for response to God's promise.

The reservation I would highlight is that a style focused so pointedly on converting the lost is an inadequate emphasis for a continued ministry to the found. It focuses more on an individual, point-in-time witness than on the outreach of infectious ongoing relationships. As the Introduction to Part 2 suggested, confrontation techniques themselves too often do not lead to sustained involvement in church life with fellow believers. Lutherans do face the challenge of developing skills to move beyond village assumptions to effectively minister in camplike social settings. But whatever the setting, basic to Lutheran identity is commitment to sustaining Christian life within a community of faith. Styles that emphasize how church life is itself a witness, in addition to confrontation evangelism, will fit better with Lutheran distinctives.

Fundamentalism presents another strain of Evangelical style. From the viewpoint of those who participate, it was described as a life-plan orientation. But Fundamentalism is not a particularly fruitful touchpoint for a Lutheran blend that will facilitate church growth. It might seem attractive because of a common emphasis on certainty grounded on the authority of inspired Scripture. But growing Fundamentalist churches usually carry that certainty farther into prescribing the specifics of Christian living than Lutheran theology can support. As I suggested earlier, the opportunity to be taught a detailed life plan from God is the key to the infectiousness Fundamentalist churches often have. Lutherans are ever cautious about preserving the focus of Christian living on justification by faith. They resist legalism too much to be convincing about a call to obedience to the will of God interpreted as a specific blueprint for the future.

Of Lutheran church bodies, Missouri Synod Lutherans have probably had the most interest in Fundamentalism. The relation between the two is explored in Milton Rudnick's study *Fundamentalism and the Missouri Synod.*[1]

CONTACT AND THE LORD'S SUPPER

Contact orientation is the name I gave to the Evangelical strain that emphasizes the experience of God's life-changing presence. His presence is celebrated through the joy, love, and power He gives. There is an inherent Lutheran resistance to basing the certainty of His presence on such emotions. But there is common ground in appreciating experiential contact as a sign that He is indeed present. That is one of the meanings of a sacrament.

Of all Christians, Lutherans emphasize the Real Presence of Christ in the bread and wine of the Lord's Supper. That is a special presence which happens when the words of God's promise of His presence, repeated at the consecration, are joined to the external elements. As Luther loved to quote approvingly of Augustine, "The Word is added to the element and it becomes a sacrament."[2]

The Eucharist is a thanksgiving celebration of God's gift of His presence in a manner that can be eaten and drunk. He touches people, and He does it through bread and wine. They in turn can touch Him; they can experience Him with their senses. This is a contact event. A sacrament is God's use of human senses to reestablish contact.

The touchpoint with Evangelicals is acceptance of the principle that God can use human experience to convey the Word of His offer of forgiveness of sins, life, and salvation. Experience alone is not the point of reference, any more than eating or drinking alone are the Sacrament. Rather, when "the Word is added to the element," to that which can be touched and felt, there God's presence is to be experienced. Feelings of joy, love, and togetherness can come from many sources. They can become shared signs of God's special life-renewing presence when they are grounded in and attributed to the Word of His action in Christ that consecrates those experiences.

I dare not suggest that the contact-oriented Evangelical church style, as described earlier, can show Lutherans new sacraments. Only those specifically ordained by God can be trusted for His reliable presence, and the Lord's Supper and Baptism have to remain central. But this style can show how sacramental thinking might be extended, that is, how God's presence can also be recognized through other forms of combining the Word of His promises with what believers can touch, feel, and experience.

Churches that stress liturgical worship have learned adeptness at extending sacramental thinking. They supplement the experience of God's presence with Word-based stimulation of the human senses: special visual symbols that strike the eye, special music to touch emotions through hearing, and sometimes even special aromas to stimulate the sense of smell. Thus such churches use a variety of contact points. The style is distinctive for appealing to believers with restrained, well-cultivated sensibilities who tend to respond to artistically refined symbols.

From the viewpoint of assessing church styles associated with church growth, the question is whether many potential new church participants can through highly developed liturgical styles find what they are seeking. Although there are many alternative explanations for the following observation, it should be noted anyway: The liturgical renewal movement became especially popular among Lutheran churches in the 1960s, and that was the decade when the numeric decline in the membership of those church bodies began.

Contact-oriented Evangelicals—"spiritually oriented," to use Hill's term—would not call their style an extension of sacramental thinking. I am suggesting that Lutherans can better understand and perhaps appreciate some of the emphases of such a style by seeing it as a simpler, less ritualistic and more populist direction for developing experiential dynamics similar to those cultivated in liturgical worship. Both stand in contrast to the exclusive Word emphasis of classical Reformed style.

LUTHERAN PIETISM

Another potential touchpoint between Lutheran and Evangelical styles is their common history.

As I noted earlier, much of current Evangelical style can be traced to roots in the 19th-century Holiness movement. That in turn drew heavily upon 18th-century Wesleyanism. John Wesley is quite explicit about the formative influence his interaction with Moravian missionaries had upon him in the time leading up to his famous and decisive Aldersgate experience of May 24, 1738.[3] These Moravians were associated with the new Herrnhut colony in Saxony that became a leading center for the Pietistic movement that was spreading rapidly among Lutheran pastors and churches in northern Europe. The colony's leader, Count Zinzendorf, was the godchild of Jakob Spener, frequently recognized as the father of Lutheran Pietism. For reasons that go beyond this formative influence, there is cause to look at aspects of Evangelical style today as a remaining Anglicized version of what Lutherans had in the Pietism of their tradition.

Pietism has come to be a negative word in most Lutheran circles today. That is generally in reaction to excesses of subjectivism, emotionalism, and legalism that appeared at various times. One interpretation of the vision propelling the liturgical emphasis of recent decades is to see it as an effort to expunge the last vestiges of Pietism from Lutheran worship.[4] Some words, intended to be negative, used in connection with Pietism are emotionalism, mysticism, subjectivism, quietism, moralism, separatism, individualism, and otherworldliness. Martin Marty's assessment, written in the 1950s, charged: "For all its glories, Pietism was one of the major strides of Christian retreat from responsibility as it has been viewed in the past."[5]

A different, more favorable assessment has been emerging in recent years, and it urges looking beyond exaggerated caricatures. Dale Brown states it most clearly in his *Understanding Pietism.* He builds on F. Ernest Stoeffler's scholarly opinion of Pietism as the most dynamic movement within Protestantism, and on Donald Bloesch's evaluation of it as one of the most important wellsprings of new life in the church.[6] Brown cites five motifs of Pietism that are distinctive: (1) concern for reformation of the church, particularly when it is bogged down in institutional rigidity; (2) emphasis on the Bible as the means for reformation; (3) insistence that orthodoxy be accompanied by orthopraxis ("right living"); (4) a theology of experience, focused on regeneration ("the God who is good enough to forgive us is powerful enough to change us"); (5) hope for the world, expressed through acts of mercy.

Pietism was without doubt a strong influence on the development of Lutheranism in America. Its father, Henry Muhlenberg, was avowedly a Pietist, sent from Halle, the domain of perhaps the best-known German Pietist, August Francke. Theodore G. Tappert traces the significant influence of Pietism on colonial American Lutherans.[7] Many 19th-century immigrants carried with them the Pietistic influences felt in the Danish Lutheran Gruntvigian movement and in Norwegian Lutheran Haugeanism. Among Swedish Lutherans the revivalist Mission Covenant movement had a lasting impact, also spawning the Evangelical Covenant and Evangelical Free churches that identify today with the current Evangelical movement rather than Lutheranism.

Pietism Among Missouri Synod Lutherans

The new Evangelical Lutheran Church in America is a merger of Lutheran churches that were themselves mergers of many synods with their own distinctive histories. The Missouri Synod throughout its history was the largest single synod, and it presents a history today comparatively uncomplicated by merged roots. This church body had its most immediate European formative experience in the Awakening movement (*Erweckungsbewegung*) in Germany in the years after the Napoleonic Wars. It was a time of "recrudescent (refreshened) pietism and orthodoxy, one time enemies, now merging and making common cause against recurrent rationalism."[8] Out of that context came the founding colony of immigrants to Missouri in 1839; they were "characterized by their intense pietism and their strict Lutheran orthodoxy."[9] Descendants in this century remember and celebrate mostly the confessionalism and orthodoxy of the 19th century, preserved in the written legacy. But Pietistic influences remained strong in the style of the ordinary church life of that century and even into the present one. This could be seen in an emphasis on personal morality and provisions for feelings and conversion experiences, although these were handled quite differently from then-current revivalistic methods.

The first head of the Missouri colony was Martin Stephan, who had been a leader of Pietists and the Awakening movement in Dresden. He was soon succeeded by C. F. W. Walther, who oversaw the Synod's growth until almost within a decade of the turn of the century. Walther's spiritual formation was strongly impacted by his student involvement in a circle of Pietists at the University of Leipzig and by the ministry of his mentor, Stephan. Another significant influence at the beginning was Wilhelm Loehe, who in the 1840s sent missionaries to the struggling Lutheranism of the Midwest from his base at Neuendettelsau, Bavaria. His youthful formation was in Nürnberg Pietistic circles that fostered devotional meetings and missionary endeavors. His missionaries carried his emphasis on practical, activist piety.

The early-19th-century Awakening in Germany produced a piety that was a revived form of 17th- and 18th-century Pietism. Many of the characteristics of those earlier forms were perpetuated in the various groups of "Old Lutherans." That designation was the preferred one among those who later learned to identify themselves with Missouri, the state where Walther had his home base and led their prime seminary.

Infectious Growth Among Immigrants

The context for development of a refreshened Pietistic style was the experience of immigration. Within the past century and a half, exciting Lutheran outreach and growth in this country has been most apparent among Lutheran immigrants and their children through several generations. It offered a church-life combination that met a strong felt need among those who first settled in the new country. It did so even among their grandchildren and great grandchildren as they migrated into the cities in the first part of this century and out to the suburbs after World War II. This style emphasized the reassurance of basic identity and familiar community for people under circumstances where they were unsure of themselves.

Lutheran historian James Albers describes the combination that was so effective for Missouri Synod churches in the 19th century. Although most who joined the Synod were immigrants and Lutheran by tradition, they had not necessarily been deeply religious in Germany. The process of immigration uprooted them from their relatively secure surroundings where religious traditions functioned well and placed them into an environment in which the uncertainties and unfamiliarities of daily life created a deeper sense of religion, often conservative in character. Caution and conservatism were generally the hallmarks of those who wished to survive in a culture which was to some extent alien. Thus a religious approach that was personalistic, emphasized personal piety and social morality, and yet continually proclaimed the presence of a loving God, fitted well the religious need of many immigrants. The fact that the religious and social dimensions of the lives of immigrants matched so well is part of the explanation for the growth of "Old Lutheran" denominations, especially the Missouri Synod.

The leaders of the Synod, themselves immigrants, understood well what their new members were experiencing and what they needed to hear. Even before they left Germany, Walther and others had passed through the valley of despair and doubt and had emerged on the other side with an evangelical faith. They were determined to build a church in which others would have similar faith experiences. Turning their backs on the German state churches, they set themselves to the task of building an American Zion that was founded on Lutheran confessionalism and a lively piety.[10]

Walther spoke for the "Old Lutherans" when he stated that Christians needed to have a profound spiritual experience, or awakening, as stated in his lectures on *Law and Gospel:*

> According to God's Word any person who has never felt the testimony of the Spirit that he is the child of God is spiritually dead. . . .
>
> Lastly, ask any person who has all the criteria of a true, living Christian whether he has experienced all the things of which he speaks, and he will answer in the affirmative, telling you that, after experiencing the terror which God sends to a sinner whom He wants to rescue, he had an experience of the sweetness of God's grace in Christ. He will tell you that his heart is melting within him at every remembrance of his Savior's love. Again, he will also tell you that, spite of the fact that he knows he has obtained grace, he is frequently seized with fright and anguish at the sight of the Law.
>
> Note, then, that our statement that no one must base his salvation and his state of grace on his feeling does not mean that he can be a good Christian without having experienced any feeling in regard to religious matters. . . .
>
> In his *Church Postil* . . . Luther . . . writes as follows: "At this point every one is to ascertain whether he *feels* the Holy Spirit in his heart and *experiences* His speaking [italics in original].[11]

RESTORING THE BALANCE

Three things are happening that are causing disintegration of the combination that made the spirit of so many Lutheran churches so infectious during their period of growth.

1. The felt needs of the natural constituency have changed. The great migrations of northern Europeans to this country are long over. The second wave of their descendants' migrations to the cities and the third wave to the suburbs are now for the most part completed. Individual families still move around, of course. But they are not part of a pattern that shapes a concentrated, shared need.

Many undoubtedly still seek assurance of security, but the causes for their insecurity are more diversified and ill-defined. The immigrant generations have been assimilated.

2. The distinct ethnic culture of Lutheranism is disappearing. Lutheran style was most effective among people who shared a common culture centered on a church tradition that was known and respected. Assimilation brings an inevitable end to ethnicity. As described in Chapter 5, tradition in general and the church institutions built from them are not so well respected among the New Believers today. The inherited cultural base that has been the context for effective Lutheran church life will carry a tradition-dependent style only with increasing difficulty.

3. Distinct styles of spiritually oriented Lutheran piety are not well cultivated anymore. This is an overgeneralized way of saying that experiential Pietistic influences have receded significantly from current Lutheran style. Partly that is because they were driven out by more formalized liturgical emphases. But that probably happened in turn because of the abatement of the need which the Lutheran Pietism fashioned in the past century was so adept at meeting. Pietistic expressions also began to look out of step with times that seemed to call for more aggressive engagement of Christians in social issues.

The various Lutheran church bodies will necessarily continue to discuss issues of their theological substance. In some respects their differences resemble the distinction between Old Lutherans and New Lutherans in the 19th century. While substance was truly at issue in some of those discussions, style differences were often predominant.

The New Lutherans today seem headed in the direction of further assimilation into the theological orientation and the agenda and style of mainline Protestant churches. They tend to look to liturgical practices and social action to set the style for their modernized piety. Neither of those two emphases, however, appears very well related to infectious church growth at this stage of religious life in America.

The Old Lutherans of the Missouri Synod have reclaimed the confessional orthodox stance that has been one basic component of this church body's substance from the beginning. But that was only one component. What will happen to the other, the emphasis on piety? Throughout this church's period of growth, orthodoxy and piety were cultivated together. Some today would seem to make the preservation of orthodoxy itself the major focus of their practical piety. But when the combination was most effective, right teaching was kept in perspective as a necessary means to developing the Christian life of response to God's saving presence. What will be the style that helps that presence be most readily recognized in today's culture and that cultivates a church life of infectious response?

A style still tuned to immigrant needs for certainty and assurance of identity is not likely to stimulate such response. Nor will a style that depends for its effectiveness on a traditional church culture that is fading from consciousness. Perhaps the emphases of an older style could be effective among the newest immigrants from non-European countries, but they hardly share the cultural presuppositions of inherited Lutheran style.

As a style which churches can cultivate, experiential "contact" Pietism has repeatedly shown its worthiness as a wellspring for new church life. It is a style that has a rightful place in Lutheran theology and history. Today it is practiced most effectively by many Evangelical churches. Lutheran churches concerned about outreach have good cause to go, look, and assess. Perhaps they may find something from their own roots that they can readapt.

PART 3

Infectious Talking and Organizing

Introduction

Back into their histories is one direction old churches should go and look for practices to renew. Sideways is another direction to go and look, focusing on practices and styles of other churches, especially the ones that are growing today. Forward is the direction the Lord lays out for us all. What are some practical insights for shaping their future church life that Lutherans can gain from a look at Evangelicals?

The most practical insights can come from concentrating on how Christians can talk about and organize their response to God's call to follow. Defining how God does the calling is a matter of church substance, and so is the setting of general expectations for how believers are to respond. Style most clearly emerges in the specifics of everyday talk and action.

A DEMOCRATIC MOVEMENT

A key to the infectiousness of growing Evangelical churches today is their emphasis on ways of communicating and organizing that stay close to the response instincts of ordinary Christians who love their Lord. Evangelicals typically are not apologetic about letting church life be simple. The strength of this simplicity does not have to do with lowering expectations for living the new life in Christ. As Dean Kelly's study pointed out, the growing churches are typically quite demanding of their participants. Rather, this is simplicity at the level of encouraging faith expressions and action responses that new believers as well as old ones can readily understand and quickly make their own.

Older churches often get used to relying for their strength on emphases that have developed over the years and have gotten to be several steps removed from the uncomplicated, relatively spontaneous reactions of new and ordinary believers as they encounter their Lord. Such emphases can be scholarship, carefully prescribed polity and procedures, centralized authority, centuries of tradition, polished liturgy, and lengthy, carefully worded confessions. As great as these strengths can be, Evangelical vitality today serves as a reminder to keep the basics of Christian living front and center. Older, declining churches might find insights for renewing their strength by looking at how Evangelical style helps that happen.

A good place to begin is with a readiness to trust and affirm the responses of ordinary believers. This is what makes the Evangelical movement truly democratic, in the opinion of Nathan Hatch. He observes that American Christianity in its Evangelical forms has not had its driving force in the quality of its organization, the status of its clergy, or the power of its intellectual life. The central dynamic has been its democratic orientation.

> In America, the principal mediator of God's voice has not been state, church, council, confession, ethnic group, university, college, or seminary; it has been, quite simply, the people. American Christianity, particularly its evangelical varieties, has not been something held aloof from the rank and file, a faith to be appropriated on someone else's terms. Instead, the evangelical instinct for two centuries has been to pursue people wherever they could be found; to embrace them without regard to social standing; to challenge them to think, interpret Scripture and organize the church for themselves; and to endow their lives with the ultimate meaning of knowing Christ personally, being filled with the Spirit, and knowing with assurance the reality of eternal life. These democratic yearnings are among the oldest and deepest impulses in American religious life.[1]

Hatch sees this style of Christianity as democratic in at least three respects: It is audience-centered, intellectually open to all, and organizationally pluralistic and innovative.

While most Protestant church bodies in America today are more or less democratic in their polity, many old ones are descended from European state churches that were far from democratic in their style. That is particularly true for Lutherans, whose German and Scandinavian cultures and state churches were highly authoritarian in previous centuries. The instinct is still to leave the determination of truth to more qualified higher authorities and to want institutional permission before undertaking individual initiatives.

Truly products of American democracy, Evangelical churches

have acted out of the impulse to rework Christianity into forms that were unmistakably popular. Whether or not a church wants to be "popular" is a real issue. The term can carry negative connotations, such as being coarse or lacking refinement and sensitivity. Taking a popular position can also mean failing to call others to account, failing to urge them to higher, God-given standards. Churches want to be right, even when that makes them unpopular. But basically "popular" means "of the people." A democratic church can be popular in the sense of relying on the people for its power. When Hatch highlights the democratic foundations of Evangelical churches, he is pointing out that they have been first and foremost people's churches.

The leaders of the earliest Christian church in the first century remained close to the people. They stayed joined together with ordinary believers while figuring out and expressing in the context of their times what it meant to be disciples of Christ. The theological foundation they laid was for a people's church. As cultures change and churches age, however, leadership efforts to preserve what was said and done in the past sometimes allow that earlier orientation to slip out of focus. Out of the newness of their church experience in the most democratic of countries, Evangelicals reflect style emphases that can help older churches get back to the vitality of a popular people's church in today's cultures.

The emphases highlighted here are clearly matters of style—the ways church people talk and the ways they organize. The discussion is aimed at helping older churches, particularly Lutheran churches, regain a style of talking and organizing that is infectious in its own way.

The first insight, developed in Chapter 9, is to concentrate on finding and building an audience for God's Word. Camp style of audience contact seems especially effective for that purpose. In Chapter 10 the emphasis is to encourage church members to express their faith in personal terms, adding their own experiences to the traditional formulations of the faith.

Organizational coherence is often a major concern as churches age. Chapter 11 urges greater openness to the decentralized and segmented style of organizing characteristic of a grassroots movement. Democratic does not mean an absence of strong leadership, but it is leadership that expects to derive its human power from the people. For churches that have settled into organizational patterns of carefully controlled access to church positions, Chapter 12 highlights the need to keep leadership a shared venture with many rather than a separate authority reserved for the minister.

Thus the following chapters suggest that old churches concentrate on:

1. More Camp Style of Audience Contact
2. More Personal Faith Expressions
3. More Movement Style of Organizing
4. More Leadership by Personal Gift

CHAPTER 9

More Camp Style of Audience Contact

Audience-centered is how Nathan Hatch describes Evangelicals. In identifying their emphasis on "the sovereign audience," he asserts: "While others [other American Christians] may have excelled in defending and elaborating the truth, and in building institutions to weather the storms of time, evangelicals have been passionate about communicating a message."[1]

Many churches are hesitant to talk about those who attend on Sunday morning as an audience. That is certainly so with Lutherans. The worry is the connotation that worship participants can be passive mobservers expecting to be entertained. The communication that happens in worship is supposed to be their work as well as that of the pastor who leads the community's expression of relation to God. Contact is assumed among the familiar faithful gathered week after week.

Out of the background of their formative camp setting for church, Evangelicals have typically not been able to make that assumption. Contact has to be initiated over and over again because of the expectation that each gathering will have new and different people. The concept of "audience" does not detract from what is going on. To deliver the message from God's Word, there has to be an audience, understood as an assembly of listeners. Getting them to listen makes audience contact a central concern. The determination to find and build an audience for God's Word shapes much of the distinctive Evangelical style of church life.

Much of the Lutheran style of communicating was shaped by Lutheranism's formative village church setting, as described in Chapter 5. For village Christians, gathering as church is a well-recognized responsibility, whether or not they find the event interesting. They come not so much to receive as an audience but to offer their service of attendance. Well beyond needing to build an audience, a village style tends to view those who gather as prepared to give their full attention to what is said and done. Words that affirm the familiar thus often take precedence over communication that arouses attention.

Consider how well they do in winning and holding audiences in the most competitive environment for getting a hearing—radio and television. The National Religious Broadcasters (NRB) is the media arm of the National Association of Evangelicals. In 1966 it listed 104 member organizations. In 1983 it had 1,000 stations or producers, made up of 922 radio stations, 65 TV stations, 535 radio producers, and 280 TV-film producers. It claims a weekly cumulative audience of 130 million. In contrast, the National Council of Churches, representing the old-line Protestant establishment, co-operates with the three major national TV networks in producing religious programs available to local stations for free public-interest broadcasting. Recently their three mainline religion series together attracted an audience that was only one-fourth the cumulative audience of the top eight independent evangelists, who have to purchase their time.[2]

I offer one illustration of the Evangelical flair for finding and holding an audience. There are millions more like it. This one is my wife. In Marcia's case they did it by paying attention to her needs as she drives the freeways to and from work. She listens to a local Christian radio station that during rush hour broadcasts daily messages from a succession of Evangelical preachers. Some are local; others have national distribution. They hold her attention day after day, even though she is a lawyer with many other things to think about. At first she was hesitant to listen receptively. She is a lifelong Lutheran, born and raised in a Midwest village church, and she retains high loyalty to her church. But what she hears meets her current needs with enough regularity that she stays tuned in.

The point is that Evangelicals show a flair for addressing the widespread felt needs of people today. In local churches as well, their communication concentrates on recognizing what ordinary people are seeking in their religious lives. This style has much of its roots in camp church settings. Indeed, modern media outreach is but an extension of camp church style.

The point is not that old churches should do better media ministries. More important is for churches to concentrate on their routine ministries done in local congregations. Few can aspire to effective media outreach. But through in-person encounters, all can more effectively reach out and hold the current and potential audiences right in their immediate vicinity.

How a gathering of believers talk about their faith is fundamental to the style of any Christian church. The point is not that old churches should learn to talk just like the Evangelicals. Their vocabulary, incidentally, is one which, because of media impact, is steadily becoming the norm for popular religious discourse, a development that in itself calls for adjustment in the communication style of leaders in churches with other histories. The attempt here is to interpret some of the emphases that can be appreciated without necessarily borrowing the vocabulary. The primary insight is that old churches can regain an infectious spirit by concentrating on the felt needs of the audiences within their reach.

Specifically the suggestions are: (1) Appeal beyond a traditional audience; (2) Make contact through personal stories; (3) Look for audience response; (4) Stay close to the audience.

APPEAL BEYOND A TRADITIONAL AUDIENCE

Gaining insights from someone else's communication does not necessarily mean abandoning an inherited style. It can lead to increased flexibility. Consider St. Paul's flexibility in style. He certainly knew how to appeal to an audience. Depending on the audience he was trying to win over, he was adept at shifting his style. We can observe how he talked to (1) a traditional audience, (2) an elitist audience, (3) an audience of ordinary people.

Appealing to Traditionalists

In the absence of technology for mass communication, Paul had to travel about in person to spread the Good News. He headed for concentrations of people. Thus he spent his time in the cities. There he usually headed first for the most sympathetic audience. Thus he did much of his witnessing in the synagogue, among people who knew and respected the tradition of the Old Covenant.

In Acts 17 we can see some of his specialized style for this audience. He was in Thessalonica. "As his custom was, Paul went into the synagogue, and on three Sabbath days he reasoned with them from the Scriptures, explaining and proving that the Christ had to suffer and rise from the dead. 'This Jesus I am proclaiming to you is the Christ,' he said" (Acts 17:2–3). We are told that some of the Jews, a large number of God-fearing Greeks, and more than a few prominent women joined Paul and Silas.

Paul's style there was effective. This was an audience that knew the Scriptures, and they were looking for the promised Messiah. Paul could show from Scripture how their well-defined need was met in Jesus, the Christ. This was content evangelism. This was also a specialized audience.

Most pastors today spend most of their time addressing the specialized audience of believers who know and respect the traditions of their church. They usually become good at a style that draws on that tradition, using it to reason about the meaning of Jesus as Savior in current life. Sometimes, however, they understandably lose perspective on how exceptional their inherited audience has become, talking with a specialized church vocabulary that has developed over the years and even centuries. Then their impact tends to be limited mostly to people who share the tradition.

The communication issue for leaders intent on expanding their church's outreach is, on the one hand, how to stay in close contact with their primary audience while, on the other hand, appealing to new audiences with a style that does not rely on previously conditioned allegiances for its effectiveness. Becoming adept at a less specialized style is particularly important as a church's traditional audience shrinks. The only compelling reason to pay more attention to other audiences is to stay effective at evangelism. But that is cause enough.

Appealing to Elitists

Paul undoubtedly felt the confines of his synagogue style. Seeking to expand the impact of the Gospel, he was drawn to the opinion leaders of the dominant Greek culture of his time. These were the philosophers at Athens. In their first contacts with him out in the city, some thought he was a babbler. When Paul witnessed to them at their meeting place, the Areopagus, he changed his style.

His approach is presented in Acts 17:22–31. He used objective reason, arguing from general principles. Observing that they did have objects of worship, he got their attention by noting that they were uncertain about God. From creation he reasoned about the God who made all things and all peoples, even determining when and where they should live. Paul did not appeal to his own tradition; he drew on Greek literature (v. 28). He ended his witness with confrontation. This God commands all to repent, for the day of judgment will come. This evangelism effort was moderately effective; some joined him and believed.

The Areopagus can be looked at as an early version of today's universities. These have become prominent cultural centers, whose doctors of philosophy are very influential opinion leaders. Especially old, mainline churches have sought to reckon with university culture, as it has shaped increasing numbers of people in the modern emphasis on higher education. Many pastors, themselves products of universities, have worked hard to develop styles that appeal to the objective reason necessarily cultivated in those cultures, as well as to the value standards promoted there.

Clearly this audience deserves serious attention for witnessing the Christian Gospel. But a style with that orientation is not without its own risks. A major one is that the substance of the Biblical Gospel message can get diluted or confused. The Pauline certainty and the call to repentance is often lost. Such concerns remain in the background of theological issues that separate conservative and liberal Christians.

The risk to be highlighted here, however, is much more practical. University-based opinion leaders are a rather limited audience. Their standards of discourse are essentially elitist. A style honed to appeal to that audience is likely to become another version of specialized communication that still does not reach general audiences of ordinary people. As near as we can tell, Paul's Athenian style brought only moderate results; there is no record of a great Athenian church in his time. There is also little evidence that a university-determined style brings infectious church growth today.

Appealing to Ordinary People

Paul before the philosophers is very different from Paul before "the people." We can observe his style for that audience in Acts 22. He was facing a crowd that had been stirred up against him as someone who wanted to change their old ways. This audience was far from sympathetic. He had to work hard for a hearing.

First of all Paul got their attention by speaking their own dialect, Aramaic. This was the common language of the ordinary people, the *laos,* or laity. "When they heard him speak to them in Aramaic, they became very quiet" (Acts 22:2). In Athens he undoubtedly spoke in Greek, the language of his epistles. In the synagogue he would have spoken the literary Hebrew in which he was so well trained. He now paid extra attention to the audience before him by adjusting to their idiom, even though it was comparatively crude.

Here he did not argue from Scripture. Nor did he reason from objective principles. He told them a story, indeed a highly personal one. It was his own story of what God had done to him. Asserting that he was a Jew of their city, he started by stressing his relationship to the hearers. He, too, had been very skeptical of the first Christians. Then he described in detail how God made Himself known to him in Jesus and dramatically changed his life. The message was that the power of God was at work in him. He was just telling about what he had seen and heard.

What Paul did is tell his born-again experience. This is the point of contact he chose to emphasize, and he even used it as his basis of authority. His synagogue style and later epistles make abundantly clear that his message had a more profound base. But he had to hold his audience's attention, and he could do so by being very personal.

Even though that day's event was not counted as one of Paul's evangelistic successes, he did get a hearing. That was the first step. He did it with a distinctive style of communication. It is a style he must have used freely in his years of missionary work. It is reflected also in his epistles, where he did not hesitate to put himself forward as a person with feelings and relationships that others could identify with. He dared to be personal.

MAKE CONTACT THROUGH PERSONAL STORIES

When I started listening to Evangelical preachers, one of my first impressions was that indeed I was listening more. My mind did not wander as much as it had during years of hearing familiar Gospel presentations, usually in 20-minute blocks. I noticed that I can usually listen to 30- or 40-minute sermons by Evangelical preachers without becoming anxious for the end.

Reflecting on differences in preaching style, I find that sermons hold my attention best when they draw on personal experience. If it is not the pastor's own experience, it is someone else's that is known and told through the speaker's personal knowledge. My observation is that Evangelicals do this frequently. Stories of personal encounters with God seem to flow one after the other. I almost always listen, and I often find myself making comparisons to stories in my own life. When I ask my wife what keeps her tuned into radio witnessing on the freeway, she assures me that the ones she likes best make Biblical truths so personal.

I notice the difference because in my own background the more customary style is to present truth more as propositions, Biblically derived. These usually come out in somewhat abstract statements about God, belief in Christ, and life situations. It is more of a deductive style of reasoning: Because of what we know about God in Christ in the past, this is what He can mean for us now. My characterization of Evangelical style is that it is more inclined to present truth in terms of the experiences of people today. This often comes out as stories of discovery and celebration of God's life-giving presence. It is more of an inductive style of reasoning: God did this to me or to John or Mary, and He can do it to you, too; here is His assurance from Scripture. Either way, the truth can be the same. The difference lies in how attention is drawn to it.

My explanation for the different communication styles goes back to the formative setting of new Evangelical churches. Their preachers could not take an audience for granted. In their various temporary, camplike gatherings, they had to quickly establish and continually maintain contact with the audience, or the people would not come back. Revivalists are usually master storytellers. Furthermore, as Nathan Hatch notes of Charles G. Finney and Dwight Moody, what was most important for them is that each person have a profound experience with God. They were cautious about anything that might produce dull and ineffective communication, including too much emphasis on formal study of divinity. "Attuned to the needs and concerns of average people, both discarded hidebound forms for new methods that would awaken the unconcerned and re-awaken the complacent."[3]

Preaching from personal experience has ample Biblical precedent. Reasoning inductively, we can find reassurance that God blessed this style in the preaching of Peter and John. After the first church grew to five thousand, the temple leaders called them to account, as related in Acts 4. They were astonished that these two were unschooled, ordinary people, but they had to recognize that they "had been with Jesus." Peter and John defended their approach by saying "We cannot but speak of what we have seen and heard" (Acts 4:20 RSV). They dared to be personal. They shared their own experience of what it was like to be with Jesus.

LOOK FOR AUDIENCE RESPONSE

One exchange I had with an Evangelical pastor helped open my eyes to audience contact. He was describing his weekly routine. Monday mornings included a staff meeting that began with a critique of the Sunday worship service. When I inquired about that, he said they evaluated each part and its sequence, such as songs and readings as well as sermon. I am used to general comments, but such systematic, detailed review seemed unusual. When I naively asked what they were looking for, the answer was an assessment of how effective each part had been. They talked about how the congregation had responded and what could be improved.

From this matter-of-fact explanation I realized how different my tradition-bound perspective on leading worship had been. I am used to worship as replication of a pattern that stays pretty much the same from Sunday to Sunday, with minor variations. There is not much to review weekly, except perhaps the sermon. Change comes in the form of selecting a differently ordered setting as it is presented in the service book. Doing the service well is of course important, but audience reaction to specific parts is usually not a major criterion of how well it went.

Effectiveness remains for me a jarring word when applied to

worship. But I am learning how to appreciate its significance as a reflection of a central emphasis in Evangelical style. A recurring theme is that each person should have a profound, personal experience with God. With that as an objective for interacting with those gathered to worship, a natural question is whether most people could indeed recognize having had such an experience. If not, what could be done differently to help it happen among more of them?

Put more positively, looking for audience response can be a matter of looking for the Holy Spirit's movement among those who are gathered. What do the worship leaders hope the Spirit will do? On a specific Sunday, are they looking for Him to heighten feelings of joy, or to stimulate more loving relationships, or to strengthen the resolve of those followers of Christ? It is not inappropriate to look afterward for evidence that God indeed blessed this time together by moving people with the Spirit in ways that had been prayerfully anticipated.

Nor is it inappropriate to ask whether the human means relied upon for the Holy Spirit's use actually helped or hindered Him. In various presentations of the Word that were read, recited, sung, or spoken, were most people able to stay attentive and apply the words to themselves? Or were parts done so boringly or mechanically that there was little communication? Did the music that Sunday help to touch emotions in preparation for the Spirit, or did most of the hearers filter it out as a neutral background; was it just entertaining without supporting a recognizable experience with God?

That Monday morning staff discussion had one other dimension that brought added incentive to the weekly review. This Evangelical pastor placed a high priority on the continued growth of his church. With the communication means at his disposal he wanted to improve worship dynamics for the audience of visitors as much as for the audience of regulars. He did not want to risk being lulled into complacency by general impressions of response from familiar faces.

Audience contact begins with an attitude toward communication, and communication can become more infectious when leaders focus on getting a response from several audiences at the same time.

STAY CLOSE TO THE AUDIENCE

One of the results of my exposure to Evangelicals is that I now hesitate about which way to face when conducting a worship service. In Lutheran liturgical tradition the pastor sometimes faces away from the people when invoking the Lord's presence or offering prayer. I find it increasingly difficult to turn my back on the audience.

A priestly understanding of pastoral leadership lies behind this stylistic practice. The leader functions as representative of the people before God, and as God's representative before the people. This mediating role can be very meaningful for those who appreciate it. But consider the implications for audience contact.

This style communicates that God is somewhere else than with everyone who is gathered. He is envisioned as present at the altar; that is where the sacrament of the Lord's Supper is consecrated and where His presence is primarily to be experienced. One implication is that other common experiences with Him are less important. Another, more practical, implication is that the leader ends up talking to what is visibly an inanimate object. In some churches the altar is part of the front wall, and the pastor then is talking to a wall. That has become hard for me to do. It accentuates a break of contact with the participants. The people themselves seem a better reminder of where His presence is to be felt. More than a communication style, facing them is a matter of respect for their importance before God. It implies no less respect for Word and sacrament but keeps the focus on what God intends to do with these means of His grace.

In terms of communication style, the priestly liturgical tradition has the effect of accentuating a separation between communication and audience. Various vestments frequently worn by the pastor help to underscore that separation. There is undoubtedly strength in the dignity and objectivity such symbolic distance adds to the worship experience. Looking with Evangelical sensitivities, though, I can better see the weakness that often appears when the formalities reinforce pastoral communication that tends to stay somewhat impersonal. Within the pastor, the style can serve to raise rather than reduce psychological barriers to close audience contact. The business suit most Evangelical preachers wear for their Sunday service reflects a different intent. To help shape their own outlook as well as that of the participants, they prefer to stress their identity with the audience, not their separation.

Beyond symbolism, the liturgical propensity for the leader to stand apart, even at times facing away from the audience, reflects a significant assumption about the leadership task. It is not so much one of building up community among those who happened to have gathered together. Rather, the pastor's focus is to express a community that already exists. Their identity as people of God is taken for granted.

In this context the concept of audience itself is cause for worry that the expectation of corporate worship as something done by the participants will be lost. But audience is an essential concept for evangelism.

When it comes to evangelism, highly developed liturgical forms suffer from an inherent weakness. This style does not lend itself well to initating fellowship. To appreciate the experience of God's presence that is offered through those forms, participants need to have extensive prior knowledge and training. The symbols themselves usually have to be experienced over time before they become conveyers of deep spiritual meaning. Unfortunately, a high liturgical emphasis can drive a wedge between the gathering of regulars who know, appreciate, and love this communication, and an audience of uninformed visitors who have to struggle to follow along, let alone to feel included. Watching newcomers struggle with a complicated service book is a sobering reminder that evangelism is at best a secondary concern in this approach.

Few Lutheran churches would ever change their style so much that the rich heritage of liturgical worship is forgotten. Yet within Lutheranism there have been periods of sometimes more and sometimes less emphasis on traditional structure and symbols. The trend of the past generation has been toward greater reliance on formalities and ritual. But that liturgical renewal has not been associated with a burst of church growth. In practice the style is often more responsive to well-reasoned needs of past believers, carried forward as tradition, than to the felt needs of current participants.

Evangelical vitality can serve as a reminder to concentrate on making and holding ongoing contact with those who are gathered as an audience for God's Word. Church leaders willing to shift their liturgy to provide more opportunities for spontaneous, informal, and personalized contact are likely to discover styles of communication that become more infectious.

A basic issue for Lutherans is to clarify with which audience to make contact: the faithful believers well prepared to appreciate their tradition, or the newcomers yet to be included. As the latter become a self-conscious priority for old churches, their efforts to reach out to them will almost inevitably bring new emphases in communication style.

CHAPTER 10

More Personal Faith Expressions

Evangelical preachers on TV and radio are there because they are unusually good at what they do. They can attract listeners by the thousands and millions. Yet public preaching is but one dimension of a church's communication style, perhaps not even the most important.

If church growth were primarily dependent on exceptional public speaking by the pastor, the growth of Evangelical churches would remain fairly spotty. In fact, much of the steady growth occurs through an increasing number of small churches. These leaders have the help of dozens and even hundreds of other active Gospel communicators. The talking that makes church life really infectious is done mostly by believers in their ordinary lives.

Differences in personal witnessing style particularly struck me during interviews to fill a seminary position for facilities manager. One of the stated job qualifications was that this person had to be a Christian. How the candidates, from a wide variety of backgrounds, went about telling me they were Christian was interesting. Some gave assurance by reviewing positions they held in a church, like trustee or choir or committee member. Others made personal statements of faith about how they had accepted Christ or what He meant in their lives.

I noticed a pattern. Those who were more comfortable talking about their church affiliation tended to come from congregations in older, mainline denominations, including several Lutherans. They in effect let others speak for their identity. Those who were at ease making personal faith statements, sometimes without even mentioning their church, had a background that turned out to be Evangelical. In matters of faith, they were used to speaking for themselves. One can wonder how much this pattern contributes to differences in rates of church growth today.

Churches can look at evangelism as something done only by a few—a program done by one committee. Indeed, in witnessing to strangers only a small percentage of Christians of any church background are consistently effective. But by far most new people come into a church's fellowship through witnessing by friends and relatives. This is repeatedly shown in studies of how churches grow. Christians could rely on talk about a church's organized programs to be their message. But their personal sharing of how they experience God in their lives is bound to be the more significant and lasting witness. Church life that encourages and supports ordinary believers in communicating their own experiences of faith is church life primed to be infectious.

How can churches, particularly old churches, encourage more widespread sharing not just of member affiliation but of personal faith? From my observation of Evangelical style I offer these suggestions: (1) Turn small talk into faith talk (and vice versa); (2) Bless simple talk, even when immature; (3) Use more "movement" language; (4) Stress shared personal prayer.

TURN SMALL TALK INTO FAITH TALK
(AND VICE VERSA)

Consider an after-church-is-over test. This occurred to me when I was comparing my usual Sunday morning experience with what I heard at Evangelical churches. It involves listening to what church members talk about in their casual conversation.

"What is God doing in your life?" is a common question in Evangelical conversation. It is taken more seriously than a polite, "How are you?" Mention of some personal joy or challenge often comes in response. "Let me tell you about this blessing God gave me last week," is another direction. Or "Pray for me, because . . . " The relationship to God gets verbalized frequently. The exchanges often involve the sharing of fairly personal concerns. The worship experience itself has a way of becoming a springboard for some of that sharing.

These themes impress because they seem so meaningful in comparison to the casual church conversation I am more used to. In the past 15 years I have been a part of three well-established Lutheran congregations. They each encouraged a coffee and fellowship time after the service. But the exchanges seldom seem to move beyond small talk that one could hear in almost any social setting—the weather, sports, business, mutual acquaintances, children's activities, things to do that day. The worship service may get mentioned occasionally, but then mostly in passing if something unusual happened.

Small talk among Christians is better than no talk. But faith talk is better yet. I know my fellow church members are people of faith, often strong faith. Occasional special conversations bring this out. But the style of ordinary weekly communication does not encourage such sharing as a routine focus of conversation. In churches with long histories and secure identity, there is a tendency to assume faith. Without regularly sharing it in personally meaningful terms, however, the church fellowship that should be a natural expression of the common faith is likely to become shallow among participants. The potential for mutual upbuilding and witnessing is inevitably reduced. In terms of evangelism, such a fellowship is likely to be less than compellingly attractive to newcomers unsure of their own faith, let alone that of others they are looking to for support.

Evangelical style has taught me a better appreciation for a part of Lutheran doctrine that is often forgotten in Lutheran practice. According to the historic Confessions of this church, there are five means of grace through which the Gospel is offered. The first four are well understood: the preached Word, Baptism, the Lord's Supper, and Confession and Absolution. The fifth was added by Martin Luther himself. The Gospel is conveyed "through the mutual conversation and consolation of brethren." (Smalcald Articles, Part III, Article IV)

Few Lutheran churches leave the first four means to chance. They carefully cultivate the ministries of Word, sacraments, and confession. Yet the ministry of "mutual conversation and consolation" of fellow Christians usually receives nowhere near the same intensity of purposeful attention. Many leaders are not even aware it is doctrinally significant. Small talk alone does not do the job. But it can become a means of grace when used to convey the Gospel. Turning small talk into faith talk can help that happen. This really amounts to bringing recognition of God's presence and grace into ordinary conversation.

BLESS SIMPLE TALK, EVEN WHEN IMMATURE

A Bible class discussion highlighted for me the reason so many Lutherans hesitate to talk personally about their faith. I was sharing some of these observations about Evangelical styles. The participants generally agreed that it was not easy for them to express their religious feelings and beliefs to others. One older man offered an explanation for his difficulty. He could not shake from memory the childhood knuckle rappings he used to get from his pastor. These happened when he made a mistake in reciting the catechism. The lesson he learned is that in religious talk it is better to say nothing than to risk saying something wrong.

He comes from a tradition where there is a right way to talk about God. It has been summarized in the written form of catechetical, doctrinal answers to the important questions. The pastor's role is to teach these answers to people, especially children. This communication style has been basic to many historical churches that are sure of their theology and want it passed on well preserved. Such churches place a high value on orthodoxy, or right teaching.

My purpose here is not to question orthodoxy. It is a great strength when it stands at the center of a church's substance. Catechetical instruction can lay a sure foundation for a lifetime of belief and understanding. I do, however, want to point to the impact an orientation to historical orthodoxy can have on the everyday communication style of ordinary Christians.

Emphasis on right doctrine can have the effect of putting faith talk into a special category removed from the give and take of informal exchanges. It can instill a fear of making a verbal mistake. For those who are not sure they can remember what they were taught, saying too little is a better alternative than running the risk of error by saying too much.

Infectious faith talk tends to remain simple. While classical theology teaches a message that is simple in essence, the formulations worked out over the centuries can make it seem complicated. Undoubtedly greater Christian maturity comes through understanding potential complications of Christian life and belief. The question is how much to talk with cautious words and concepts that anticipate the complications before they arise. Too often, simple faith talk then becomes a casualty. It seems immature, particularly when adults do it.

The challenge is how to bless simple heartfelt faith talk while offering the correct teaching that can strengthen it. The two forms of communication can get out of balance in older, matured churches. There, simple faith talk, like that often heard among adult Evangelical Christians, can seem childish. Intent on maturity, leaders of such churches are often quick to see all sorts of ways to improve or correct what may be inelegantly or naively said. Against the standards of intellectually mature theology and an integrated world view, such talk is indeed often childish. But in terms of communication style, is that a strength or a weakness? Evangelicals tend to make it a strength. These ordinary believers feel free to talk about their beliefs, at whatever stage of faith life they may be in. Whatever the other implications, their witness can be easily understood by others.

The tension is not unlike that highlighted by Jesus when He was teaching in the temple on Palm Sunday, as recorded in Matthew 21. What He communicated was so simple that a crowd of children got excited. With the words "Hosanna to the Son of David" they shouted their faith. The chief priests and teachers were indignant. They felt these followers should know better than to be so noisy and naive, especially in the temple. The leaders wanted to know if Jesus approved. He did. Jesus reminded them that God blesses praise even from the lips of children. Earlier the grown-ups had been saying the same thing the children did. I do not think the Lord blessed their simple talk any less.

USE MORE "MOVEMENT" LANGUAGE

"When I became a Christian" is a favorite phrase of Evangelicals. It is said as a lead-in to some other comment about a personal discovery, a change in relationships, or some value that became very important. An individual B.C. and A.D. of personal history—life before and after the experience of salvation—becomes a unifying thread woven through even casual discussions. As I write this, I recall a comment earlier in the day from a seminarian I chatted with at the service station. He was putting a date to a scary experience due to neglecting his car brakes at a time "before I was a Christian."

Ordinary conversational focus on the life-changing impact of salvation should be a source of satisfaction to a pastor. But the phrase can be very upsetting to some when it is used by men and women who were thought to be Christian all their life. How can someone who was baptized as a child, raised by committed Christian parents, and nurtured and confirmed by a caring congregation calmly talk about "when I became a Christian in college"? Such an implicit put-down of Baptism and youthful church life can seem offensive.

This phrase opened up insights for me when I challenged its use by several Evangelicals who I learned had conventional Lutheran upbringing. They acknowledged that, yes, they had been a Christian in a general sense. But their religion did not mean as much to them as when they "became a Christian" later. They were not describing an abstract category. They had experienced a new level of personal meaning. That is the turning point they want to talk about.

I no longer rush to correct the doctrinal implications of what could be viewed as a simplistic understanding of faith. I was able to affirm the positive side of their experience when I began to realize that they are speaking a different language, even though the words sound familiar. I am used to religious language that assumes a status before God that, through faith, does not change. Evangelicals prefer to speak a language of movement, sharing experiences of changes that, through faith, continue to happen. Another of their favorite phrases is "spiritual journey." Evangelical style includes frequent reviews of a person's spiritual journey. It leads to engaging storytelling.

Becoming Bilingual

These are different languages. One is more abstract and states truth as propositions. It is the language of doctrine, offering careful distinctions and clarifying understanding. The other is more concrete and presents truth as personal discovery. It is the language of experience, celebrating new life as it unfolds. Less precise, it may be confusing to others, but it expresses meaning for those who speak it.

One of the difficulties leaders of older confessional churches have with Evangelical preachers is that they often do not understand the language. Even some of the more visible representatives of Evangelical style have not taken the time for the formal study of theology. This is not as important to them and their churches. They cultivate the language of experience. They will often willingly agree that their theology can be refined and improved. But for their communication effectiveness they rely more on their personal expressions of faith. Appreciating the strengths of that style of witnessing can help temper the criticisms of its weaknesses.

For Christians used to formal theological language, being more supportive of personal faith expressions amounts to becoming bilingual. One language is better than the other for a given purpose. Doctrinal language remains essential for a firm foundation. But experience language is helpful for sharing the transitions that add personal meaning to the life of faith. One describes what growth in Christ should look like. The other describes how a believer has actually grown. Adeptness at both styles is important for communicating the Gospel.

"When I became a Christian" is not likely to become a conversational phrase in churches that affirm infant baptism. One of the challenges for Lutherans is how to recapture more of the personally expressive terms, phrases, and images that fit within its historic confessional vocabulary. The Pietistic periods of previous centuries excelled at emphasizing this kind of language. Hymnody from those periods can be a rich resource for those who want to be bilingual Lutherans.

STRESS SHARED PERSONAL PRAYER

Prayer is the believer's most basic expression of personal faith. It is also a key to faith talk that becomes infectious. How Christians pray shapes the way they express their relation to God and what others see of their faith. Prayer also has a lot to do with how the Holy Spirit strengthens believers for infectious witnessing.

While all Christians pray, they do not all pray the same way. Through my association with Evangelicals, I am struck by differences in prayer style.

What is usually modeled in Lutheran church life is carefully constructed prayers that are thoughtful and often beautiful. These are liturgical prayers, usually read for and sometimes by those joined in worship. As in other parts of church life, most of the praying is done by the most skillful person present, usually the pastor.

These practices make good sense. But I have become more conscious of the impact they can have on ordinary believers. Prayer becomes a special act done by somebody else. Of course all are encouraged to do it for themselves. But among Lutherans I do not see that being done very much. One is left to assume that fellow believers talk to God on their own, but there is often little evidence. Some churches are left with the sort of situation I experienced one Sunday morning filling in for a vacationing pastor. No one else could be found who was willing to offer the prayer at a congregational breakfast after the first service. They had to depend on the visiting professional to do it for them.

Among Evangelicals spontaneous individual prayers without written preparation seem to arise with regularity. Sometimes this happens in a conversation, and sometimes those prayers are even long ones.

Such style of prayer contributes to infectious faith talk in several ways. It is the exercise of a relationship with God that demonstrates personal meaning which others, too, can have. More hesitant Christians presumably also have that relationship through their faith. But those who are ready to talk out loud to God in everyday language about everyday matters are also giving a powerful form of witness.

The prayer I see is more personal in another way. It frequently names others for whom God is thanked and His care is sought. It seems to me that I have been prayed for by name more often in my few years among Evangelicals than in most of my adult life among Lutherans. The implications for building fellowship are significant. It is easier for someone to feel closer to Christians who publicly remember him or her before God than to Christians who seldom get around to sharing such an expression of care.

Practice for Evangelism by Talking to God

A church that models shared personal prayer is doing much more for witnessing than communicating personal meanings of faith. It can actually help prepare believers for direct evangelism. Prayer can be the easiest starting point for overcoming hesitance to express faith personally.

Churches can chose from many available techniques for teaching members to witness to others. While valuable, such programmed techniques run the risk of letting evangelism appear more complicated than simply sharing what a believer has experienced in Christ. One of their basic objectives is to help believers overcome their hesitance or fear of talking to others about the Gospel. Most intimidating is communicating religious truths and experiences to strangers, especially if the one doing the witnessing is worried about finding the right words. A technique orientation has a way of underscoring that witnessing is not something that comes naturally.

Preparation for evangelism is easier when Christians become accustomed to hearing and giving expression to personal faith with the flow of routine communication among sympathetic fellow believers. Frequent opportunity to share personal prayer provides that kind of communication. Churches whose members are not accustomed to talking with others about God's action in their individual lives are churches that will predictably have difficulty with an expanding evangelistic impact.

But even such sharing within the fellowship can be difficult for churches whose inherited style of communication does not support it well. The easiest starting point for becoming more confident in expressing faith personally is to talk freely and often to God. God is the most sympathic hearer. He wants His people to pray to Him and express their beliefs, discoveries, and experiences, as well as their fears and concerns. Verbalizing this relationship is the most fundamental preparation for finding the words and courage to talk about God to others.

Lutherans usually have little disagreement that they do not personally express their faith as freely and confidently as many other Christians they meet. While explanations abound, there is usually little inclination to defend this reticence, especially among those who are concerned about extending the outreach of their church. Lutherans will always be concerned that they communicate the full Scriptural substance of the Gospel message. What they can learn from Evangelicals is how to personalize their talk about its meaning.

Concentrating on enriching the fellowship life of shared personal prayer is the most practical step toward more infectious faith talk, even more practical than learning evangelism techniques. But the main reason for emphasizing personal prayer as a key to evangelism is what it does to individual believers. It brings them constantly before their Lord to let Him shape their daily experience of following Him. Through prayer based on God's Word, believers keep open the way for the Holy Spirit to work the personal experiences of faith that give Christian life its special meaning—the meaning that is so exciting to share with others. There is always room to improve personal prayer life. Communication style with others will take care of itself when the relationship with God is well exercised.

CHAPTER 11

More Movement Style of Organizing

"Movement" is a featured term in the vocabulary of modern Evangelicals. They talk a lot about the "Evangelical movement" and where it is going. In his scholarly overview, George Marsden suggests distinguishing Evangelicalism as a movement from its identity either as an emphasis on characteristic doctrines or as a defined set of institutions.[1] As noted in Chapter 4, the movement is the most likely source of helpful insights for other church bodies.

One of the characteristics of a true movement is that it is hard to define and is typically not well organized. This is both a strength and a weakness.

The weakness is that onlookers have a hard time coming to grips with it. What, precisely, should they look at, and who should speak as its proper representatives? Established mainline church bodies have been quite willing to carry on dialog with other churches. Thus, for instance, there are ongoing discussions between Presbyterians and the United Church of Christ, or between Lutherans and Roman Catholics as well as Episcopalians and Methodists. Each of these bodies has formally organized, denominational-level representation and can designate appropriate spokespeople. To date there has been little formal dialog with Evangelicals. One of the reasons is that there is no clear counterpart denominational organization.

This situation could be viewed as an organizational lapse in need of remedy. But it is better viewed as a basic feature that is a strength and which presents a source of insights for the more highly organized church bodies. One can observe that a basic reason Evangelicals are in a period of vitality and growth is precisely because they are not well organized in the pattern of a national church body. Rather there is a tremendous multiplicity of separate groupings, ranging from very small fellowships to very large bodies, that are energetically pursuing the vision of mission and ministry most compelling to them. While they have much in common, they typically develop few formal ties. Yet they retain a loose kinship.

Mainline churches have difficulty understanding the Evangelical movement because of their own particular history of using the "movement" concept. The word is not strange to them. Most of them participated enthusiastically in the "ecumenical movement" that was the focus of so much attention in the 1950s and 1960s. But that occurred especially at organizational levels of church life, among designated leaders, who looked for ways to bring various traditions and organizations closer together. Ordinary Christians at the congregational level were usually not involved. A common observation in the 1980s is that this movement has lost much of its vitality. One explanation is that it lost touch with the practicing Christians it represented, and that could happen because of the focus on higher-level organization.

The alternative to a centralized style of organizing is not just an absence of organization. Any joint effort that has continuity has structure of some sort. The Evangelical style is that which is associated with a popular, grassroots movement, one that stays close to the people involved, in all their diversity.

MOVEMENT STYLE OF ORGANIZING

Anthropologists Luther Gerlach and Virginia Hines offer a framework for understanding how such movements are organized. They studied popular American movements of the 1960s, particularly the Pentecostal/charismatic movement. They highlight three features: The overall organizational structure is highly decentralized, highly segmented, and highly dependent on informal personal and event linkages (reticulation, in their terms).[2]

To say that a common effort is decentralized is to say that there are many scattered leaders who exercise a considerable latitude in decision-making within their own sphere of influence. Within movements such leaders emerge when others recognize that they have something valuable to offer; a formal process of voting or appointment is secondary, if present at all. This sort of decentralization means that no one person speaks for the movement. In Evangelicalism today, for instance, it would be difficult to find agreement on who the top 10 leaders are.

Such organizing is decentralized because movements are usually highly segmented. They have a great variety of localized groups or cells which are essentially independent and are in the process of dividing and recombining. Often the groups do not have formal membership. In this style each unit has different ideas about how to achieve its objectives and has its own interpretation of what it is doing. These starting points of local groups adapting to their own situation and needs give a movement its special ability to spread to new people and different cultural groups. In terms of infectious evangelism, such a high degree of fluid segmentation seems to be a key organizing principle.

What holds all this together? This is the basic question of church leaders who are used to more formalized, centralized membership and voting structures for carrying on their joint efforts. The answer for movements is that linkages are maintained mostly through personal ties of leaders as well as participants who recognize that they share with others a commitment to a common cause. These informal ties are supplemented by special events, like revivals, that bring participants together and affirm their common identity. Special-purpose national associations often provide opportunities for such events. Currently the National Association of Evangelicals, the Evangelical Press Association, and the National Religious Broadcasters can be recognized as serving that purpose for Evangelical leaders.

While the movement style may seem far distant from the church life of highly organized established Protestant mainline denominations, it is part of the formative history of most. Christianity itself began and spread as a movement that developed only a loose organizational structure in the first century. In its beginnings the Reformation was very much a movement. One way to read its history is as a reaction to a Roman Catholic church organization with a tight structure that had become too far removed from ordinary Christians. Presbyterians and the United Church of Christ can trace much of their roots to the populist Puritan movement in the 17th century. Methodism is a product of the populist Wesleyan movement in the 18th century.

Lutheranism is a special case because it so quickly took the form of centralized, closely monitored state churches. Early on, Luther and the other movement leaders looked to princes and kings for protection, and in many of the German states as well as in the Scandinavian countries that was readily granted. The disastrous Peasants' Revolt brought an end to populist movement dynamics. An emphasis on formally appointed leaders under higher-level supervision is deeply imbedded in Lutheran tradition. So is dependence on formal institutional ties between congregations. The Lutheran Confessions are the explicit linkage that holds them together. A European heritage of pastors salaried and disciplined by state authorities was a major ingredient in shaping a strong tradition of valuing a uniformity of belief and practice that goes beyond the formal organization in place at any time.

It would be naive to suggest that Lutherans today could ever shift their organizational ways completely over to a movement style. But that does not mean there is little to learn about organizing from the Evangelicals. Lutherans can learn to become more confident about reacting to movement dynamics when these do occur. This would involve resisting the instinct to tighten up church body organization in the face of change and new styles of ministry. The fundamental insight is to be more willing to let innovation and adaptation happen at the level of ordinary Christians and their natural groupings. Then worry about organizing it later. Along with this can come more willingness to trust that a common effort will emerge from commitment to a common cause.

Specifically, in this chapter I will highlight what greater segmentation could look like for Lutherans. The next chapter looks at more decentralized leadership. Shifts in leadership style would have to emerge from Lutheran understandings of the office of the ministry and the priesthood of all believers.

The segmentation emphasis should not be a new concept for Lutherans. For most of its history Lutheranism in actuality has been quite segmented. In Europe this occurred among language and geographical groupings. There never has been one centralized Lutheran church body. In America those groupings became even more segmented by immigration patterns diffused over the vast expanse of the new country. There were dozens and dozens of Lutheran church groupings and synods. Nineteenth-century American Lu-

124

theranism can be seen as demonstrating movement dynamics among German and Scandinavian immigrants.

In this century the instinct for higher-level organization has been a dominant concern among most American Lutherans. This has taken the form of one official merger after another, culminating in the major merger forming the Evangelical Lutheran Church of America. Arguably, one result has been less openness to the sort of grassroots segmentation that keeps church life adaptive and innovative. At a minimum this emphasis has kept leadership attention several steps removed from the basic gatherings of Christians where infectious growth most naturally occurs. It remains to be seen whether this style of organizing helps the participating church bodies turn around the decline in membership they have experienced in recent decades.

Significantly, The Lutheran Church—Missouri Synod has chosen to retain its distinct identity by not participating in mergers throughout its 140-year history. It is opting to stay segmented now. While there has been a strong centralizing tendency in synodical organization in the last several decades, the formal polity remains distinctly congregational (unlike, for instance, the former Lutheran Church in America). This is a polity that at least in theory lends itself to a lively segmentation process. It is the Missouri Synod which most shares the conservative causes and theological emphases of the Evangelical movement. Greater openness to the organizational style of Evangelicals can perhaps be a significant factor in a new burst of infectious spirit in this church body.

Here are some specific Evangelical emphases that can be highlighted in Lutheran organizing: (1) Structure around primary fellowship participation; (2) Accentuate local church initiatives; (3) Affirm parachurch organizations; (4) Recognize the blessing of diversity.

STRUCTURE AROUND PRIMARY FELLOWSHIP PARTICIPATION

One of the first things a Lutheran has to learn when looking at Evangelical churches is to count differently. A church of 300 means two different things. For Lutherans it expresses membership, usually counted as adults and children (communicants and souls). The difference goes beyond whether to include children. For Evangelicals membership itself is not the key factor. Participation is. Thus a church of 300 means that 300 people are usually involved in the weekly Sunday activity. They constitute the basic fellowship that is active in the primary functions of the church at any time.

The difference is most apparent between Lutheran and Assembly of God congregations. Sunday attendance for Lutherans usually averages a third to a half of the membership, and in some of the older churches it may be only a quarter. In Assemblies, membership is often only half of those who participate. This designation is reserved for those who make a special commitment. Of two churches with Sunday attendance of 300, the Lutheran may talk about membership of 1,000 and the Assembly of God may give the membership as 150.

What lies behind this distinction? A difference in emphasis between a church as fellowship and a church as organization. A fellowship is a process of sharing something in common; it happens when a person participates in the sharing. The Book of Acts describes that more specifically, as it says of the first Christians at Pentecost: "They devoted themselves to the apostles' teaching and to the fellowship, to the breaking of bread and to prayer" (Acts 2:42). In practice, Evangelicals focus on prayer and the study of Scripture, and they are generally willing to consider anyone who is involved in these basic activities as part of the fellowship, however informally. The emphasis is on active participation. An Evangelical Christian is likely to talk about "being active" at a named church.

Lutherans are more likely to talk about "belonging to" a given church, which they "join." Theologically, that congregation is a fellowship in the most fundamental sense. But as the approach to numbers suggests, it is a fellowship a person can be part of with very little, if any, active participation. It often becomes symbolic membership in name only. In effect, the fellowship takes on the characteristics of a volunteer organization—a formalized relationship among those who are carried on a membership roster. A one-time public confession of belief is the necessary step for "joining." While frequent attendance is of course encouraged, it is not essential for inclusion.

There are certainly strengths to this tradition, with its roots in the parish orientation described in Chapter 5. A parish organization puts itself on record as wanting to provide spiritual care even for those whose commitment to church life is slackening. A weakness, however, is that this emphasis on the formalities of membership tends to lead to an emphasis on organizational involvement when promoting participation in church life. The primary fellowship acts of devotion "to the apostles' teaching . . . and to prayer" can become secondary.

An exchange I had with a Lutheran pastor highlighted the practical difference between concentrating on secondary organizational dynamics in comparison to primary fellowship dynamics. I had been talking in a conference about Evangelical prayer practices. He expressed his frustration at trying to incorporate more shared prayers in the life of his congregation: When groups did that first, they often did not adequately get to the business at hand; but when they had prayer time after the meeting, the evening got so late. I asked him why they tried to do both lengthy prayer and business at the same session; how about having a separate evening prayer session? But he worried that an extra evening would mean expecting many of the same people to be at church almost five nights a week. My response was that there must be something wrong with the way the church is organized. Where is their time better spent—in sessions of shared prayer or in committee meetings?

Committees, boards, and organizational routines have a way of becoming the dominant church activities for the minority of Lutherans who participate in something more than Sunday service (and those attenders are often already a minority of the membership). For the average Evangelical church, small groups for Bible study and prayer are the more dominant structured activity. In fact, in some thriving Evangelical churches the central worship service has less attendance than the various small groups combined.

A look at church physical plants can show the difference. For Lutherans the sanctuary is usually larger than the adjoining small-group meeting spaces, which are mostly occupied by children's Sunday school. For Evangelicals the common meeting area is often overshadowed by the collection of rooms and buildings for adult as well as children's groups. Such a physical structure expresses a high priority for groups small enough for everyone to participate in.

The point of these observations has to do with style of structuring church life. Movement style reflects segmentation of participants into relatively small groups that feature interaction around the primary activities that express and support their commitment. For Christians the fellowship sharing of God's Word and mutual prayer are about as basic as any church life activity can be. While committee duties are certainly necessary in the formal church organization, a gathering of Christians that lets such secondary activities become the main focus of participation beyond the Sunday celebration is depriving itself of important fellowship dynamics that sustain an infectious spirit.

Lutheran tradition carries at least three constraints that need to be addressed in becoming more open to this style. One is a historic resistance to relatively independent small fellowship groups in a congregation—negatively labeled "conventicles" or *ecclesiolae in ecclesia* (little churches in the church). The worry has been mostly one of maintaining control, a concern that is much less significant in movement-oriented churches. Another constraint is the widespread hesitance many Lutherans have to express their faith informally in personal terms. How to address this was discussed in the previous chapter. The third constraint is difficulty mobilizing small-group leaders. This leadership issue is discussed in the next chapter.

ACCENTUATE LOCAL CHURCH INITIATIVES

What one means by "the church" becomes a reflection of organizing style. My ears are used to hearing "the church" describe an entity which covers regions, countries, and even the world. Thus there is something called "the Lutheran Church" that includes millions of Christians who share the common denominator of the Lutheran Confessions. The church is much larger than the local congregation.

Among Evangelicals it took my ears quite a while to get used to hearing "the church" used in the narrower sense of just the local congregation. Lutherans would say "the parish," but that village-based term does not transfer to the camp church setting of Evangelical history. What I had taught as parish administration became church administration. At first I thought it necessary to emphasize that I would deal only with the congregation, not the denominational administration. But that was taken for granted. Finally it dawned on me that for most Evangelicals "church" is virtually synonymous with "congregation." The larger groupings are generally associations of churches, and they are typically of much less interest.

Such higher-level organizing of churches is of less concern because of the ready assumption that the real action occurs at the level of the local church. Each congregation is inclined to take upon itself the responsibility to adapt to the needs, strengths, and interests of the Christians who have gathered around this local focal point. Evangelical (local) churches tend to be self-reliant units that generate their own initiatives and emphases rather than waiting for programs or organizational initiatives to come from someplace else. This style is inherent in organizing as a movement and is one of the keys to the infectious energy these churches can generate.

A result is that vibrant Evangelical churches typically appreciate and stress originality. They and their leaders are inclined to experiment with internal groupings and outreach efforts until they find the right "fit" for their situation. There is good reason to worry about carrying such self-reliance to an extreme. Dan Baumann's book *All Originality Makes a Dull Church* is a reminder to Evangelicals that the commitment to originality can cause them to miss benefiting from the wealth of experience available from other churches, present and past. Yet the experience of others cannot be as effective a motivator for action among Christians as their immediate experience of working out their own expressions of shared response to God's call. A commitment to initiative and originality is important for sustaining vitality.

Paralleling this organizational emphasis is the inclination of individual Evangelical Christians to assess their participation in church life according to their fit in a local church. For many, denominational affiliation is hardly a factor in choice. Thus one can meet long-active Evangelicals whose spiritual journey includes participation in churches of four or five denominations. Such denomination hopping is increasingly becoming a fact of church life in American Protestantism, even beyond Evangelicalism.

In contrast, Lutheran tradition is far removed from accepting minimal attention to the larger denomination as an attitude to be blessed and encouraged. The heritage of common confession and the time-tested practice of thousands of congregations is a central strength that will never be lightly regarded. Openness to Evangelical style, however, can lead to some shifts in emphasis within that heritage and its organizational expressions. The question is whether the emphasis will be on the larger organization, with the congregation as its local outpost or chapter, or whether it will be on the many diverse local churches, with the district and national units in more of a support role to stimulate and guide local adaptations.

Historically, Lutheranism has functioned both ways. As a denomination, the former Lutheran Church in America opted to stress regional units under the somewhat centralized administration of a bishop; that unit retains ownership claims to congregational properties. This pattern will continue in the merged church. By official polity and supporting theology, The Lutheran Church—Missouri Synod recognizes congregational autonomy. In theory the larger denominational unit is an association that independent congregations can join, support, or leave at will. In practice, the denomination has historically wielded great influence over congregations, shaping their efforts into a powerful unified witness. But that has been more by common consent rooted in shared ethnic cultural roots than by forced organizational compliance.

The real issue, however, is not polity. It is how much latitude to recognize for an organizational style that features congregational initiatives to shape and adapt their own ministry to the strengths and needs of their own situation. Especially in the Missouri Synod, there seems to be more official latitude than has been practiced. The nature of this church body is certainly to focus on unity in terms of doctrine. Clarity on this anchor point can itself be a significant facilitator of originality and diversity in ministry application. Knowing the doctrinal commitments that bind them together, Lutheran congregations can concentrate on different practical innovations that express their own individuality and sense of mission. Segmentation born of such confidence can help keep them close to the energizing dynamics of a church with a movement style.

One way or another, all church bodies structure relationships at three levels: small fellowship groupings within a congregation, the congregation as an organization, and congregations organized in relation to one another. Within infectious grassroots movements the informal small groups usually stay primary, and their formal structure as a multicell local organization remains a secondary concern. Regional and national connections between these local units usually get tertiary attention. Over time, however, older established church bodies have a way of inverting that order of emphasis. Primary attention gets directed more and more to identity and unity within the larger denominational structure. The local church becomes a secondary expression or extension. Getting members to participate in the basic person-to-person informal fellowship relationships then becomes a third-level concern calling for a deliberate effort often accomplished only with difficulty. By that time the infectious growth of a movement is more of a memory than a reality.

The thriving Evangelical movement can stimulate Lutheran and other old-line churches to reexamine their original priorities. It is a reminder to accentuate the local church and to concentrate on structuring it around primary fellowship participation.

AFFIRM PARACHURCH ORGANIZATIONS

One of the reasons Evangelicalism can seem almost bewildering to other Protestants is that so much of it spills beyond the familiar local church/denomination structure. There are thousands of incorporated organizations concerned with aspects of the Evangelical cause that are not directly tied in with conventional church bodies. Their number is expanding steadily. The term "parachurch organization" has become popular for describing this category of effort. It usually means an organized special ministry that is not under the direct control or authority of a local church or denomination.

Well-known youth-oriented ministries are Young Life and Youth for Christ at the high school level, and Intervarsity Christian Fellowship and Campus Crusade at the college level. The Navigators had an early focus on ministry in the military, and Jews for Jesus has its clear thrust. Occupational groups, like the Christian Legal Society and Christian Dental Society, abound. Billy Graham Crusades, Inc., sets a pattern for evangelism. Missions are the goal of most parachurch organizations. The *Mission Handbook* lists 620 North American overseas agencies, the vast majority of which are outside denominational boundaries.[3] Especially well known are World Vision International and the Wycliffe Bible Translators. In addition, hundreds of publishing efforts and media ministries should be noted. The Christian Ministry Management Association promotes improved administrative practices and skills among parachurch organizations. It has a mailing list of over 5,000 interested agencies.

The current proliferation of Evangelical parachurch organizations is not a new phenomenon in the history of the Christian church. It is an expression of the dynamics of a popular movement, and such movements and organizations have appeared repeatedly over the centuries. Most of the many orders in the Roman Catholic Church started as parachurch organizations, many having their origins in 13th- and 14th-century renewal movements. Within Lutheranism the Pietist movement of the 18th century spawned a proliferation of *Stiftungen* (institutions) for charitable purposes in addition to mission societies. Nineteenth-century English-speaking renewal fervor brought forth such nondenominational mission agencies as the China Inland Mission as well as such organizations as the American Bible Society, the American Sunday School Union, and the Young Men's Christian Association.

Parachurch organizations have always presented a dilemma for established denominational structures. On the one hand, their strong religious motivation and their ability to mobilize resources to address a focused vision clearly accomplish good things in the work of God's kingdom. On the other hand, they pose a risk to congregations and denominations which by their very nature are all-purpose church organizations.

Jerry White, executive director of the Navigators, identifies the key issues. Churches risk having their people, especially the leaders, diverted away from their own activities. Parachurch organizations often appeal to the financial resources of members, thus siphoning dollars away from church programs into what can become duplicated effort. From a pastoral perspective, intensive involvement in exciting special-purpose groups can distract members from their responsibilities to the full scope of Christian activities. Perhaps most troublesome is the question of ambiguous accountability to necessary church authority. A church risks losing loyalty to its doctrinal and spiritual discipline among members who are deeply involved in churchlike organizations acting on their own authority.[4]

The natural organizational response to risk is to seek to reduce it by asserting control over the factors that pose it. This tendency is very strong in Lutheran tradition. While Lutherans have their own array of special-purpose organizations (for example, Lutheran Youth Encounter, Lutheran Laymen's League), these are typically monitored closely by denominational structures. Program thrusts are usually carefully delineated and boundaries are protected to keep competition and duplication at a minimum. This is a sensible arrangement to conserve energy and preserve identity. It is an organizing style that fits with strong denominational loyalties.

But while reducing risk, this controlling style can also reduce inherited strength if it blocks avenues for the grassroots initiatives and innovations that generate renewed energy and fresh commitments among participants. Parachurch efforts can be valuable enterprises that stay at the cutting edge of missions, evangelism, and other forms of ministry. In large business corporations as well as churches, bureaucratic centralization mitigates against entrepreneurship and can lead to stagnation if little room is left for participants to pursue new interests and opportunities as they see them.

In economic terms, church life does not have to be a zero-sum effort, where resources are limited and time or money spent in one direction deprives other efforts of support. Churches experience infectious growth by multiplying resources. With their ability to mobilize participants, parachurch organizations can help do that in ways that stimulate the basic church units as well. The Evangelical movement undoubtedly has so many special-purpose parachurch organizations because it is in a period of bustling spiritual vitality. But, then, it is also a thriving movement because its organizational style permits and draws energy from such decentralized, segmented participation.

The question for Lutheran church leaders is not whether they should consciously try to inaugurate new ministries under separate authority. That is not the way effective new parachurch organizations typically start. They emerge from the bottom up, from the initiatives of strong-willed individuals, often lay people, who have a vision that reaches beyond the institutional commitments of established churches.

Rather the question is what attitude to take toward such new organizations when they do emerge and appeal to members. Should the first instinct be to resist them until they are brought under control? That is the safe attitude, and it is very understandable when a church body is trying to conserve dwindling resources. But it is shortsighted, *especially* when a church body is experiencing decline. A better instinct for churches intent on regaining momentum is to welcome and affirm fresh bursts of focused ministry when this occurs in their midst. Then they can work on developing cooperative relationships with these organizations so that commitment to mutual goals will grow.

RECOGNIZE THE BLESSING OF DIVERSITY

Organizational structures are human arrangements. Churches rightly try to pattern their structures according to Scriptural principles. But the Bible does not present an organizational manual that can be copied and implemented. Over the years Christians trying to be faithful in scattered groupings develop and selectively remember conscious decisions about how they will relate to each other, and the result is tremendous variance in church organizational style.

Inherent in organizing, however done, is striving for the best balance between unity and diversity. Through the apostle Paul, the Lord does lay out some relevant principles to be recognized by His people. To begin with, their unity is already an accomplished fact. It is not something they have to make happen on their own. More or less of it is not the issue. Those whom God calls to be His own become members of the body of Christ (1 Cor 12:27). In Christ there are not many bodies, but one. "The body is a unit, though it is made up of many parts; and though all its parts are many, they form one body. So it is with Christ. For we were all baptized by one Spirit into one body—whether Jews or Greek, slave or free— and we were all given the one Spirit to drink" (1 Cor. 12:12–13).

With this firm conviction, diversity is something that can be appreciated and is not a blight to be overcome. While some differences are rooted in selfish, sinful human natures, Paul teaches us to be ready to look for God Himself as the Source of a wide range of compelling interests His people can express: "Now there are varieties of gifts, but the same Spirit; and there are varieties of service, but the same Lord; and there are varieties of working, but it is the same God who inspires them all in every one" (1 Cor. 12:4–6 RSV).

The basic organizing challenge in the body of Christ is how to accommodate this diversity and help keep it contributing to the common good. This is the Lord's intent. "To each is given the [different] manifestation of the Spirit for the common good" (1 Cor. 12:7 RSV). The difficulty with so much diversity is that it sometimes seems to distract from the common good more than to contribute, according to the perspective that emerges in the real-life organizing of priorities and resources that is the stewardship responsibility of churches. The constant temptation is to make the parts fit by limiting the differences and seeking uniformity.

Some styles of organizing place so much emphasis on the organizational responsibility to promote the common good that uniformity becomes more highly valued than diversity. This is a general tendency among the older, established churches with accumulated commitments that need focused attention. It is historically a pronounced tendency among Lutherans. The nature of this church is to value uniformity of belief. But that substance mandate can too often carry itself over into a style of expecting uniformity of gifts, ministries, and energies.

A necessary reminder is that an infectious spirit of church growth and vitality can happen only through the working of the Holy Spirit. Preaching the Word and administering the sacraments are the means by which He comes, and assuring that this is done faithfully is a basic organizational task of churches. But when He does come, He enters individuals and can be unpredictable in the ways He pushes them into action. "All these [different manifestations] are inspired by one and the same Spirit, who apportions to each one individually as He wills" (1 Cor. 12:11 RSV).

In the dependence on the Holy Spirit, the right question when organizing churches is whether the style that emerges properly respects the diversity He inspires. There is always room for improvement in accommodating what the Spirit is ready to start through all sorts of believers. Popular church movements can help established churches remember what they are looking for.

CHAPTER 12

More Leadership by Personal Gift

A church's style of organizing becomes an extension of its approach toward leadership. Who are the leaders, and how do they become that? How is leadership exercised? Does it tend to be centralized among a few or spread widely among many? Certain approaches or styles lend themselves better to some purposes than to others. What style seems related to infectious church growth in American culture today?

The apostle Paul gives a fundamental teaching on church leaders and their task. It is in the fourth chapter of his Letter to the Ephesians. After he urges those believers to "make every effort to keep the unity of the Spirit through the bond of peace" (v. 3), he states the theme which is stated in expanded form for the Corinthians. Each member of the body was given a gift of grace as the Lord apportioned it (vv. 7–8). In particular, he gave "some to be apostles, some to be prophets, some to be evangelists, and some to be pastors and teachers" (v. 11). The purpose is "to prepare God's people for works of service, so that the body of Christ may be built up" (v. 12).

Interpretation of this passage lends itself to differing leadership emphases, which are reflected in the differing organizing styles of churches today. One emphasis is that Christ enables some believers today to be especially effective at fulfilling these functions in the Body, especially evangelizing, pastoring, teaching. Wherever He raises them up, these believers and their particular ministry are His gift to the church. Another emphasis is that the gift is not so much the persons as the positions God provides for the Body. To care for His church God instituted the office of ministry, with special authority and responsibility for those who hold it. Churches generally depend both on person and position in their leadership. Yet in practice one of these can receive greater attention than the other, resulting in different styles.

Style differences also emerge around a short or a long listing of kinds of leadership that are recognized. Some churches concentrate on the Ephesians 4 description and make it even shorter by concluding that apostles and prophets were given only to the early church. Others are more ready to affirm the importance of additional forms of leadership, such as healing and administration, which are included by Paul in the extensive listing of God's gifts to His church in Romans 12 and 1 Corinthians 12.

By tradition, Lutherans in their style have preferred to focus attention on institutional leadership understood in a narrow sense. The office of ministry is the key concept. Historically this means primarily pastors and teachers. Through custom, these well-established leadership positions include fairly firm expectations for the persons holding them. Lutheran churches have other positions, like elder, deacon, or trustee. But these are typically understood to be of lesser importance and are less demanding. The exercise of leadership consists mostly of fulfilling the expectations of customary positions to which individual believers are called or appointed by the gathered body. This is essentially an institutional perspective, where careful stewardship of God's gift of delegated authority is accorded precedence over the initiatives which individuals might be inclined to contribute.

Basic to the organizing style of Evangelicals is a broader understanding of leadership. It focuses much more on the person than the position. The offices of preaching and teaching are not of as much concern as the functions of preaching, teaching, and meeting the many other needs of a group of Christians. Whoever can perform these functions effectively is recognized as a leader, and the evidence is how much of a following he or she can gather. More than the office, God's gift is diverse believers who are especially enabled and driven by the Spirit to present the Word convincingly and to mobilize His people for a particular form of action. Leadership is expected to be a gift of individuals who may or may not be in positions of formal authority.

Evangelical churches are accustomed to an organizational flexibility that can accommodate strong personal initiatives. This is what helps give Evangelicalism the movement characteristics of decentralized leadership and segmented groupings, as noted in the previous chapter. The willingness to let leadership expand rather than to seek to limit it also helps explain the continuing vitality of the movement. The temporary camp church organization forms the background.

This chapter suggests that Lutherans can regain some of their earlier infectiousness by becoming more receptive to leadership by personal gift. This need not mean abandoning the institutional emphasis on office which has been such a great strength in solidifying and conserving Lutheran church life over the centuries. But it does mean a willingness to complement that emphasis with the strength of engaging a fuller measure of God-gifted individual leadership that may not fit within traditional structures.

To move toward a better balance between leadership by office and leadership by personal gift, here are some steps to consider: (1) Appreciate two Lutheran traditions of ministry; (2) Expect widespread leadership initiatives; (3) Ease access to ministry positions; (4) Be less reliant on organizational solutions; (5) Expect strong pastoral leadership.

APPRECIATE TWO LUTHERAN
TRADITIONS OF MINISTRY

Flexibility in looking for church leadership is present in Lutheran tradition to a greater extent than often realized. There is room for an understanding of both office and function. The key concept is "ministry." While the noun has its own Biblical definition as the word for service, in Lutheran practice it has taken on the general meaning of the exercise of leadership in churches. Church people look to "the minister" for leadership.

Historian James Pragman offers a very helpful overview of differing emphases in his study of Lutheran *Traditions of Ministry*.[1] He traces how the doctrine of ministry has been understood in both a broad and a narrow sense. The broad sense of ministry includes the exercise of the priesthood of all believers as well as the public (that is, institutional) ministry of the church. The narrow sense is usually synonymous with the public, pastoral ministry. I will make some interpretive comments about these traditions as they relate to the leadership question at hand.

That gatherings of believers will look to a leader to have primary responsibility to minister Word and sacrament among them is usually understood as a necessity in almost any church tradition. The Lutheran instinct is to place great value on the Pauline principle of doing things with decency and order in matters relating to the designation and oversight of the pastoral minister. Lutheranism was born out of a highly institutionalized (that is, organized) church in a well-regulated society, and it quickly sought to restore an established order in its church life. The pivotal point of control was ordination, the conferring of leadership authority in a church. As Melanchthon wrote in Article XIV of the Apology to the Augsburg Confession: "On this matter we have given frequent testimony in the assembly to our deep desire to maintain the church polity and various ranks of the ecclesiastical hierarchy, although they were created by human authority. We know that the Fathers had good and useful reasons for instituting ecclesiastical discipline in the manner described by the ancient canons."[2]

This early commitment explains much of the narrow focus on leadership set apart by carefully controlled ordination granted by authorities outside the local church, even though this polity was "created by human authority." There is no doubt that God wants well-recognized leaders in His church and that He cares for His people through this arrangement. Teaching and preserving the importance of such a special ministry is basic to the central tradition of Lutheranism. Orthodox theologian Johann Gerhard summarizes this dominant understanding of church leadership: "The ministry of the church is a sacred and public office, divinely instituted and committed to certain men through a legitimate calling that they, equipped as they are with special power, teach the Word of God, administer the sacraments and preserve discipline in the church to promote the conversion and salvation of men and to spread the glory of God."[3]

The question that gives rise to a second tradition is whether this work of ministry remains the province of those who hold this special office or whether it is a responsibility shared by all believers in the church. The dominant tradition carried a strong tendency to see it as conferred to the officeholders. This happened in the context of a centralized, state-controlled church that much preferred to recognize and financially support the leadership of just the ministers it had properly ordained.

The second strain of Lutheran leadership tradition, however, features a powerful doctrinal basis for a broader sense of ministry. Its origins go to Martin Luther himself and his discovery of the priesthood of all believers proclaimed in 1 Peter 2:9. In his 1523 treatise *Concerning the Ministry,* addressed to Bohemians trying to put order into the leadership of their reformed church, he asserted that what is essential is the function of preaching the Word and baptizing, and not the issue of who does it. Thus the father of a household can perform these functions as a member of the universal priesthood. Luther proclaimed that indeed the office of preaching is the highest office in the church, but then he added that by right and command it belongs to all believers. All ministries of the church belong to all Christians because they are each individually priests before God.[4]

Luther taught what can be called a transference doctrine of ministry or church leadership. While all believers have equal rights and responsibilities before God, all cannot preach, baptize, or perform the ministry functions within the Body at the same time. For the sake of good order they should transfer their individual priestly authority to someone they agree on to act in their stead. As Luther stated: "But because all have the privilege, it becomes necessary that one, or as many as the congregation pleases, be chosen and elected, who in the stead and name of all, who have the same right, administers these offices publicly, in order that no revolting disorder arise among God's people and the church be turned into a babel."[5]

Designated ministers are thereby servants of those who called them and who retain the final responsibility for their ministry.

This broad view of ministry was clear to Luther. Significantly, it does not receive much mention in the approach to ministry set forth in the Lutheran Confessions. As Pragman points out, the priesthood of all believers lay somewhat dormant during the later confessional period and the formulation of Lutheran orthodoxy in the 16th and 17th centuries. Then the Pietist period of the late 17th and early 18th centuries brought it to the fore again. It became one of the ministry cornerstones of the Pietists' approach to renewal at a time of slackened interest in church life. The reasons were as much practical as theological. With customary Lutheran loyalty to the established order, early Pietist Philip Spener cited this advantage: "No damage will be done to the ministry by a proper use of this priesthood. In fact, one of the reasons the ministry cannot accomplish all that it ought is that it is too weak without the help of the universal priesthood. . . . If the priests do their duty, the minister, as director and oldest brother, has splendid assistance in the performance of his duties and his public and private acts, and thus his burden will not be too heavy."[6]

Narrower understandings of ministry later reasserted themselves. But Luther's view of ministry based on the priesthood of all believers again reached formal prominence in one branch of Lutheranism transplanted to America, specifically in the formation of The Lutheran Church—Missouri Synod. C. F. W. Walther made it the doctrinal basis for the leadership authority of ministers who were at that time cut off from the ecclesiastical hierarchy of established European churches. Once that authority was in place, however, Walther and his colleagues were not inclined to explore very far the implications of his rediscovered view of ministry, even though it remains a foundation for this church body's ecclesiology and polity.

An overview of Lutheran traditions of ministry, like Pragman's, makes apparent that there were different emphases, and these emphases emerged in response to the condition of the church as it faced changing needs. The broad sense of ministry was important at the beginning of the Reformation, in the period of intensive renewal led by the Pietists, and among the "orphaned" Saxon immigrants in Missouri. The narrow view dominated when the church was inwardly strong and intent on preservation, which was most of the time.

Are Lutheran churches looking for renewal today? In the American culture of the last several decades Lutheranism has not been maintaining its strength. The theme of this book is that regaining an infectious spirit for growth is really a renewal process of getting back to the basics of church life. Where that is the desire, Lutheran history suggests what to emphasize in leadership expectations—a view of ministry that starts out as the work of all members. There is precedence for a broad view of leadership—done decently and in order.

It would be foolish to suggest that Lutherans could ever go as far as some in the Evangelical movement who are ready to affirm and follow the exciting leadership of any persuasive believer without worrying much about whether such a ministry is properly recognized by a church. As Pietists in an earlier age believed, renewal among Lutherans has to happen within loyalty to the established order. The issue is how to harmonize the emphasis on the office of the ministry with a greater openness to the contribution of believers with special personal gifts of ministry. Ideally position and person should fit neatly. Certainly the persons in the major positions should be gifted by God for this work. But a church is better poised for renewal when it is ready to recognize the presence of more God-gifted leaders than fit into the customary positions. The challenge is to shape the office flexibly enough to include the contribution of as many believers as possible who show they can function as leaders in ministry. This need not amount to downgrading the office of the ministry.

The first step in that direction is to address the status of the members commonly known as the laity.

EXPECT WIDESPREAD LEADERSHIP INITIATIVES

"Laity" is a word that does not appear much in Evangelical vocabulary. Nor does the companion term "clergy," which is a basic identifier for the leadership of old churches with European roots. Furthermore, one seldom sees an Evangelical pastor wearing a clerical collar, the badge of clergy status.

The reasons touch basic leadership instincts. As highlighted by Nathan Hatch (see Chapter 9), Evangelicalism is primarily a democratic movement, with popular or people's churches. Since laity means "the people," it could be called a lay movement. But that term would show a bias, as if there were something missing because these believers did not have proper clergy leadership. What the avoidance of a clergy-laity distinction really means is that Evangelicals expect their leaders to emerge from among the ordinary believers and to stay in close contact with them. There is inherent resistance to a formal status-consciousness that would permit some within the Body to think of themselves as belonging to a special leadership class above the rest. Reaction against inherited social class structures is part of the formative history of many Evangelical denominations. They arose out of commitment to take the priesthood of *all* believers very seriously.

The strength of this orientation is the way it primes Evangelicals to expect leadership from many rather than just a few in their fellowship. This populist emphasis is underscored by a fresh reading of St. Paul's Romans and Corinthians passages about God's gifts to His church, not just the Ephesians passage. If each member of the Body is given a different "manifestation of the Spirit ... for the common good" (1 Cor. 12:7), as the Spirit apportions these gifts "to each one" (v. 11), then every member has something to contribute. Indeed, by preferred interpretation these gifts of the Spirit are not just something given to a person, like talents or aptitudes. These are gifts to the large body ("for the common good"), brought about by the Spirit's work of moving individuals to contribute what they can do. Paul gives many examples, which are not clearly delineated in these three passages, and which read much more like functions performed than positions filled.

Evangelicals are inclined to take Paul's words to the Roman church at face value. He reminds them: "Having gifts that differ according to the grace given us, let us use them" (Rom. 12:6 RSV). Here are his examples: "If a man's gift is prophesying, let him use it in proportion to his faith. If it is serving, let him serve; if it is teaching, let him teach; if it is encouraging, let him encourage; if it is contributing to the needs of others, let him give generously; if it is leadership, let him govern diligently; if it is showing mercy, let him do it cheerfully" (Rom. 12:6–8). All of these contributions take personal initiative, which each is encouraged to exercise, moved by the Holy Spirit. Such initiatives are themselves leadership in the broadest sense. Some are more directly related to the traditional role of pastor, like teaching, exhorting, and prophesying (telling forth God's will). But there are more gifts than can be included in any one role, particularly when the 1 Corinthians 12 examples are added.

Paul's thrust is that God's people should expect ministry initiatives to be widespread in the Body. This assumption brings with it an attitude of encouraging a diversity of leadership from many sources in a church rather than trying to confine these initiatives to just a few designated leaders.

In itself the clergy/laity distinction does not force those who use it into low expectations for the contribution of the laity. But that is often the consequence. The underlying message frequently received is that those who are not clergy are somehow second-class citizens in the church. Their contribution is not so important and therefore not so necessary to exercise. Churches that make a point of distinguishing between clergy and laity usually do so because of their history in cultures of previous centuries. These are generally the old-line churches that are most worried about the declining participation of their members. How much of that worry is due to low expectations subtly communicated through the category of "laity"?

A question for Lutherans is whether they want to continue talking about "the laity" or "lay ministries." Why first tell believers they are somehow not a real minister, and then experience the typical frustration of getting them involved in contributing their own forms of ministry? While deeply imbedded in Lutheran tradition, the concept of laity need not be inherent in Lutheranism. The necessary concern is that leadership be recognized in an orderly fashion and that some be chosen for the times when ministries of Word and sacrament are done in behalf of all. But these ministries are only some gifts, however central, among many that the Lord is ready to give His people. Lutherans believe that God wants His people to be sure there is a well-recognized place for believers gifted to be pastors and teachers. These need not be viewed, however, as a separate class somehow distinct from all the rest.

Moving to a greater expectation of widespread church leadership is for Lutheranism a matter of moving beyond the village church social setting of its roots. In a stabilized village of lifelong residents there really was a class structure that set the representative of spiritual authority for the parish apart from the rest. The minister often also served as head of the village. Avoiding leadership conflict among members was highly desirable, since these people had to live together for years to come. Careful control was necessary. Keeping the spiritual head set apart aided respect for authority. Occasion for conflict over determination of leadership was reduced by the practice of having higher authorities send a carefully chosen pastor from some other locale. The term "clergy" is derived from the Greek *klēros* and designates an allotted portion, or the person to whom a portion is assigned. The "portion" was thought of fundamentally in geographic terms—the parish, which was the church gathered within certain geographic boundaries. The clergy were the church leaders assigned by a hierarchy to well-defined positions of authority in parish churches.

Evangelicals today live a church life that is far removed from village-style assumptions. The camp setting of temporary gatherings of believers who expect to move on was their formative experience. Control was not as important as initiative. A strong sense of mission to neighbors who were not already gathered in a church provided plenty of opportunity for leadership in ministry that did not have to be closely monitored, as in a village. Finding little Biblical precedence for a class structure they resisted anyhow, they were inclined to think of themselves as fellow laborers in the Kingdom, without a need to distinguish between clergy and laity. They thus set the expectation that ministry was work every believer could and should do. Here was a style that lent itself well to unleashing a wide range of personal gifts God was ready to give.

This section could be called "Make More Use of Lay Ministry." But that would perpetuate a dated notion of dubious value in church life today. "Expect Widespread Leadership Initiatives" makes the point more clearly.

EASE ACCESS TO MINISTRY POSITIONS

If a believer is personally moved by the Spirit to take an initiative in ministry, how long should he or she wait to be asked by others before exercising that gift to the Body? The way churches answer this question says much about their style and its relation to infectiousness.

Out of their camp church orientation, Evangelical believers are inclined not to wait long at all, either because they find opportunities within their fellowship or because they receive encouragement to head out on their own. A man or woman who "feels a burden" or who is "moved by the Spirit" to share the Word may start a Bible study group or a small prayer group within the church. The stories are legion of those who sacrifice security to do the outreach work that starts a group or a new church they lead as pastor. They know they are called to leadership when they have followers. This attitude toward personal initiative that does not wait shapes the organizing style of decentralized leadership and segmentation that is characteristic of movements.

By instinct Lutherans are much more cautious. They usually prefer to have a more organized process of formally recognizing someone as leader before accepting that person's initiatives. This is perhaps a German or Scandinavian cultural characteristic in general as much as it is an outcome of the village church setting. A result is that in this style of church life believers gifted by God for ministry are expected to wait until a position is clarified for them, even when financial support is not involved. Worried about authority, Lutherans tend to look for permission before acting. This attitude can produce a style where church members hesitate and wait until their church formally gives them a green light. Much of Evangelical vitality comes from believers expecting to see a green light and exercising a ministry until stopped by necessity.

The difference in attitude struck me particularly when I was doing a series of workshops on problem solving in the church. Part of the format called for participants, usually pastors, to break into small groups and to work on a problem in their church that concerned them. It was instructive to hear what they talked about. Lutheran worries were usually variations on the theme of how to get more energy and participation in some aspect of church life—for instance, how to get more Bible study groups going, or how to get more youth involved. Among Evangelicals I noticed a pattern of concern that could be described as how to handle too many initiatives; they tended to worry about maintaining unity among members who wanted to go in so many different directions in their ministries. Either type of problem merits concern. But one is more likely to bring infectious growth than the other.

The difference became most apparent in a workshop with a group of church planting leaders of the Southern Baptist Texas Convention. I knew I was in a different environment when I heard their commitment to starting 200 new congregations a year in that one state, or 2,000 in 10 years. That is a goal far removed from the experience of Lutheran church bodies that do well to start several dozen new congregations nationally. Attitudes toward evangelism can help explain some of the difference. But a major difference involves expectations for access to leadership, specifically access to the pastoral ministry of a local congregation. For Lutherans, as well as other mainline churches, believers are recognized as able to exercise pastoral leadership only after completing a lengthy post-college seminary education—a long and expensive period of waiting that only a very small number of members are able to go through.

Throughout their history, Evangelicals have not relied on carefully controlled certification of this sort. While increasingly desired, a seminary degree is not looked on as a necessity for performing pastoral functions among a gathering of Christians. Demonstrating that one has a personal gift for preaching, teaching, or pastoral care remains basic, and that can be demonstrated by actually exercising such leadership. Evangelicals tend to believe that God distributed those gifts widely among His people, and they are ready to keep to a minimum any barriers to the exercise of those gifts. That is how they can envision rapid expansion of their outreach.

Lutherans value control and organizational unity too highly to ever be fully comfortable with the rather freewheeling ways of Evangelical initiatives. Recognizing the strength of this emphasis on position and organization, the question raised by looking at Evangelicals is how willing Lutherans can become to grant permission for leadership readily rather than reluctantly. When members feel led of the Lord to engage in ministry, can they be helped to find more green lights than red ones? That can happen as churches become more flexible as to how participants are called to leadership in their midst. Certainly the formal process of designating key positions, defining responsibilities, and electing officeholders will remain basic. But there can be greater organizational openness to extending informal standing to those who feel called to some form of ministry. Blessing only what is centrally organized will conserve energy. But increased church energy is more likely to emerge by learning how to bless personal initiatives first and then figuring out how to organize and guide such leadership.

Church planting presents a special challenge to Lutheran expectations about leadership. Are there additional ways to test giftedness for pastoring a congregation besides insisting on a full graduate seminary education? This challenge is particularly significant in the ministry of reaching out to cultural groups where so many years of higher education constitute a very high barrier to leadership. Readiness to ease access to pastoral ministry rises in importance as Lutherans resolve to extend their understanding of the Gospel beyond their own ethnic heritage with its distinct culture of leadership expectations. Can Lutherans be flexible enough in organizational style to entrust the guidance of other-than-seminary-trained pastors to conventionally certified leaders who remain a step or two removed from direct involvement in the ministries that are expanded in this fashion?

BE LESS RELIANT ON ORGANIZATIONAL SOLUTIONS

In oversimplified terms, the Lutheran style of organizing leadership seems driven by a strong desire to avoid the possibility of negatives happening in the life of the church. It becomes heavily reliant on careful organization to achieve such preservation. Evangelical style, in contrast, seems more ready to capitalize on the positives, particularly those that arise from individual strength and vision. They are less reliant on overall organization to achieve the building of a fellowship that is such a priority.

For instance, one of the negatives that Lutherans are necessarily keen on preventing is false teaching. Doing so becomes a fundamental organizational task, pursued by subscription to common confessions and by certification of teachers. Evangelicals also carry a passion for truth as God reveals it in Scripture, which they are conservative in interpreting and taking at face value. Yet assuring correct understanding is for them less a responsibility of the institutional church than of individuals as they search Scripture on their own. Confident of what they believe, they are typically not so concerned about organizational protection of their teaching. Getting along with diverse personal applications is the more compelling concern.

My point in this observation is not the relative importance of doctrine. Rather it has to do with different attitudes toward what organizations should accomplish among believers. From the viewpoint of caring for the church at large, Evangelical individualism seems fraught with possibilities for confusion and seems remiss in structuring safeguards against bad things, like error, that can occur in Christ's body. Lutherans seem instinctively to resist the possibility of confusion by organizing to prevent it. Martin Luther himself personified that visceral need for good order, as reflected in the earlier quotation that Christians should properly elect their leaders "in order that no revolting disorder arise among God's people and the Church be turned into a babel."

While the appearance of disorder in the Evangelical wing of God's people may seem "revolting" to Lutherans, the real question is how it looks to God. Does minimally organized individualism stand in His way of calling people to faith in Him, of enlivening those who follow, and of extending His kingdom through them? A recurring theme in these observations is that God is indeed able to work His will through this style—not just despite poorly organized leadership but perhaps even because of it, at least as evidenced by the expanding impact He appears to be granting. His direct control seems adequate to compensate for the missing human controls other parts of His church would prefer.

Another recurring theme is that the challenge for Lutherans is not so much to abandon their strengths but to temper and balance them with other strengths. Such a balance would mean finding ways to bless the somewhat messy ministry contributions of believers acting out their personal giftedness for leading phases of God's Kingdom work. Leaning in the direction of accommodating these initiatives would mean becoming more reliant on believers and congregations to develop their own good order and being less reliant on denominational processes to determine preferred solutions for how church leadership will be exercised.

The personal initiative of one Evangelical, Leighton Ford, presents an instructive example of an understanding of organization that weaves itself around leadership by personal gift. Billy Graham's brother-in-law, Ford ministered for years on the Graham staff. He served as chairman of the Lausanne Committee, a group of Evangelical leaders who organized the 1974 Lausanne Conference in Switzerland. This was a key movement "event" that launched unprecedented worldwide coordination of evangelism strategies and philosophy by conservative Protestant church leaders. In 1985 Leighton Ford formed an organization with the primary purpose of finding and encouraging young Christian leaders. He brought about a 1987 conference in Singapore for 350 young leaders from all over the world, and a 1988 "Leadership '88" assembly of 2,200 young Evangelicals in the United States. These were opportunities for giving visibility to a new generation of leaders and to help them build their reputations for what they can contribute to the Evangelical cause. The hope is that they will be more readily recognized and accepted as replacements for the older generation. All this is prelude to a second world evangelization conference anticipated for Lausanne in 1989.

This approach would strike most Lutherans as rather ambiguous and therefore something about which to be cautious. Who, precisely, is the authorizing body and what does this sort of program stand for? There is no clear answer because this is a coalition effort, made up of both church and parachurch leaders, who may or may not be participating with the formal endorsement of an established organization. But that does not bother Evangelicals, because institutional formalities are not as important as a compelling cause and the affirmation of those who can exercise personal leadership through their giftedness.

What sort of positions will these young leaders be groomed for? That is also ambiguous. Undoubtedly some will wind up in leadership positions with existing Evangelical churches and organizations. But few would be surprised if new organizations emerged to address specialized needs with a new vision—and different gifts.

What are the qualifications for participation? Invitations will be controlled, but the process is likely to appear confusing. Educational or ordination certification undoubtedly will not be necessary. Recognition of some personal leadership success in the Evangelical cause will. This will not be so much a search for leadership through institutional political processes as through general recognition of those who demonstrate special personal giftedness. They will rise in leadership as they attract more who are willing to follow.

How comfortable could Lutherans become with this sort of approach? It is not mentioned here as a model to be emulated. Lutheran history and commitment to institutional infrastructure is much too different to suggest that leadership selection could ever be enthusiastically entrusted to a process so imprecise. It is presented, though, as an illustration of a shared commitment to recognize and guide high levels of competence for ministry within a context of tolerance for ambiguity. Tight, centralized organization is not the only effective means to guide church life. In their own way, Lutherans can become more willing and creative in affirming leadership by personal gift, even when it does not emerge as clearly channeled through established leadership positions.

EXPECT STRONG PASTORAL LEADERSHIP

When I first started sharing observations about Evangelicals, I suggested rather clumsily that Lutherans could learn to place less emphasis on the office of the ministry. What I wanted to highlight is what I have discussed in this chapter—looking at leadership in ministry as functions that many God-gifted believers can perform rather than concentrating on it as a special, divinely instituted office held only by a few. What I discovered is a fear that such a shift would detract from the importance of pastoral authority in a congregation. There was even concern that this would produce weaker pastors rather than helping them to be the strong ones a church needs. Authority was already difficult to maintain.

But a weakened pastorate is by no means a necessary consequence of looking beyond the traditional Lutheran concept of the office of the ministry. That becomes apparent from observation of Evangelical churches. More the norm than the exception are pastors who wield a very high degree of influence in the fellowship and are accorded much respect as authoritative spiritual leaders—to a degree that sometimes seems excessive to Lutherans. In discussions this is sometimes pointed out to me with a tone of denial to the main point, as if there is a contradiction between a widespread sharing of ministry functions and strong pastoral authority.

Two observations can help reduce the tension between these emphases. One is that a church need not be a static entity with a fixed amount of leadership for established routines and groupings. To share leadership in such a setting would mean that the more one person takes the lead, the less others can. In general, Evangelical churches expect many participants to exert increasing influence on each other and on outreach efforts. To the extent that leadership can be quantified in terms of effectively influencing the behavior of others, there is usually more of it going on in Evangelical churches than in Lutheran. This is what gives them so much of their intensity and vitality. Thus, sharing leadership widely amounts to elevating expectations for ministries carried out by many and need not subtract from what the called, ordained minister can contribute. In fact, when ministry activity in a church is increasing through the efforts of many, the importance of strong pastoral leadership grows.

The second observation concerns where pastoral authority comes from. Does it flow from the office or from the function of ministry? Both are involved, of course, although for Evangelicals the office is usually not so carefully defined as for Lutherans. But while office can provide access to leadership opportunity, it does not assure leadership effectiveness. That usually has to be earned—by faithfully fulfilling functions of ministering to the needs felt by those who would follow. Authority becomes stronger as people willingly grant it to someone. Reliance on the rights of office is likely to produce ministers who are more officious than effective. Often the talk of professional ministers about the office of the ministry can sound like an attempt at job protection, like an effort to get around the reality that leaders must earn the support of those to be led!

Much of Lutheran history happened in a culture that emphasized how authority was conferred through properly constituted office. Regulation of church life by state authority bolstered that assumption. But current American culture seems much less prone to confer authority on a leader out of respect for the position held. Political commentators frequently discuss this development. In Lutheran circles, worry about weakened pastoral authority may really be a reflection of the effects of this cultural change. The office of the ministry undoubtedly does not nearly so easily get the same respect it once did.

The question is not whether pastors should be strong leaders, but how. The Evangelical style seems more closely attuned to this culture. Their experience can show how pastors become strong not by relying on the rights of office, but by actually touching the lives of people with the ministry they perform. Pastoral authority grows through changing lives by sharing the Word. The more pastors can help that happen through whatever gifts God has given them and others, the stronger their pastorate and the church will be.

Conclusion

Change is hard. It is hard enough for individuals as they experience and adjust to transitions in their personal, family, and work life. Change is especially hard for institutions, where transitions are often less dramatic and where many, many individuals have to work out adjustments.

Change is risky. It raises the possibility that former hard-won accomplishments may be lost, or at least not recognized. The change process can focus attention more toward the uncertainty of the future than the reassurance of the past.

Is change necessary? Because it is hard and risky, this question is unavoidable. Careful answers are also necessary because not all change is wise and good. The special task of leaders is to discern the path of wisdom amid different possibilities for the new.

Churches have to confront change. They, too, go through transitions and cycles with similarities to those of individuals and other organizations in society. The chapters in this book have addressed the possibilities for change in God's church of this day, especially in historic churches that have more at risk.

Church and change are not an unnatural coupling. The Gospel is all about the granting of new life, which churches can have as well as individuals. Indeed, God's track record is one of working continual change in the expressions of church He has granted over the centuries.

CHALLENGES FOR CHANGE

Challenge is the necessary prerequisite to wise consideration of possibilities for church change. A challenge is a call that anticipates a response. Change becomes compelling only as a response to challenge that is heard and accepted.

Challenge is what Jesus gave His very first disciples when He said, "Come and see": Look at the possibilities for change. That is

153

the challenge He still delivers today, as He continues to be a mobile and versatile Lord who keeps moving on among different people in different ways. Chapter 1 focused this challenge. The first disciples were ready because they were asking a question, "Where are you staying?": What differences will You make in life? That is the underlying question for us today. We can ask variations of it in the planning processes that get us ready for responses to His continuing call.

Challenge is what Jesus gave His original disciples, and us today, when He said, "Follow me." Christians know that call well. But the real challenge comes in the words that surround it in Mark 8: *Deny yourself and take up your cross. Be ready to lose your life for Me.* Chapter 3 interpreted that as being ready to change—to give up dependence on ourselves and to take risks, indeed big risks for the Lord. This is a challenge to the churches of His followers as well as to them individually. In confronting change, churches have to continue asking themselves how much risk they are willing to take for the sake of the mission the Lord gives them.

The fundamental challenge to Christians and their churches is presented in this assigned mission: "Go and make disciples of all nations." Sometimes easy, this task often turns out to be difficult. As noted in the Introduction, this is often because of reliance on formerly effective patterns of church life and approaches to outreach that now perhaps are less helpful in clarifying the meaning of the Gospel message for those who do not yet know it. The ongoing call to make disciples of *all* people produces the recurring need to evaluate and change methods that are becoming ineffective among the many to be reached. This response amounts to moving beyond temple thinking and finding faithfulness in a tabernacle church that goes to where the people are, as suggested in Chapter 2.

Challenge is what the numbers present. Old church bodies, including Lutherans, are in a period of decline in membership. Something they are doing is no longer as effective as before. It is not the Gospel that is in decline. God's kingdom is still alive and well in this world, as can be seen in the growing numbers of believers coming into it today worldwide—and particularly in the newer Christian churches in America. These realities call for a response from old-church followers committed to the basic mission with its built-in expectation of growth. To recognize and make sense out of church dynamics associated with decline and growth was the intent of the chapters in Part 2.

Confronting these realities, His followers today need to hear again Jesus' challenge to them as they prepare to go: *Wait for the power from on high.* First get equipped by the Holy Spirit for the work ahead. Highlighted in Chapter 4, this is the message of Luke's presentation of our Lord's final challenge.

STEPS FOR CHANGE

Challenges to churches confronting change call for response. Here is a summary of steps suggested in the previous chapters.

Step: Confess churchly failures. Lutherans believe in confession as the necessary preparation for the service of worship. It should also be so for mission service. We have but earthly vessels to carry God's treasure. In Christ God forgives our human failures, and He gives renewed life for renewed effort—to churches as well as to individual believers.

Step: Draw a clear line between substance and style—between what a church cannot change and what it can. Confidence in theological substance can bring exciting freedom in styles of worship, Bible study, social service, and outreach. This allows the celebration of changed styles while preserving necessary substance.

Step: Do not make it difficult for other people who are turning to God (Acts 15:19). In other words, draw the line around no more substance than is necessary. This apostolic injunction should inform any mission strategy a church adopts.

Step: Go and look where God's kingdom is coming with power (Mark 9:1). When mission is involved, looking at what other churches are doing need not be an act of unfaithfulness to one's own, particularly when those to be examined are growing Christian churches where the one true God seems to be at work with special power. Churches have more resources for doing this than individuals. They can go and look as they pursue careful planning processes for evaluating potential changes.

Step: Borrow from church styles that God seems to be using especially well today. Skillful borrowing seldom means replicating exactly what someone else is doing. Faithfulness to a church's God-blessed, unique heritage usually means adjusting new styles to make an appropriate fit with the old.

Step: Improve church styles of talking. Cultures and their languages are constantly changing, and communicators have to change with them. The apostles were not afraid to adjust to different dialects to get their message across (Acts 2:8). For Lutherans, improved talking lies in the direction of becoming more comfortably bilingual—using the language of personal experience of God's presence as well as the language of doctrine about His presence.

Step: Improve church styles of organizing. Scripture leaves the specifics of the church organizing process a matter of style. Organization—and its means of recognizing leaders—is a human tool to be evaluated by its effectiveness. As needs and context change, which they constantly do, the patterns of relationships between believers and their leaders in small groups, local churches, denominational grouping, and special-purpose agencies have to be continually assessed—and improved—in the light of overall effectiveness in the church's mission.

Step: When in doubt, go back to the basics. Where God grants it, church renewal can seem complicated and confusing. But it happens best when leaders stay focused on the basics of Christianity. These begin with letting the simple Gospel message have its impact—the message that has been enough to sustain churches through all the ages, whatever the complications and circumstances. They revolve around staying "devoted . . . to the apostles' teaching and to the fellowship, to the breaking of bread and to prayer" (Acts 2:42). Wherever Christians are doing that, God can do great things.

Step: Pray that the church catch a new vision. The first church of Christ began when God poured out His Spirit to give men and women, young and old alike, new visions and dreams of what life as His followers could be (Acts 2:17). Such vision unleased a tremendous burst of energy—and brought many changes. God is ready to grant a special outpouring of the same Spirit ever anew. When and where is His choice. The choice for the people of His church is how to get ready. Praying for His coming is the tried and true way:

> Come, Holy Ghost, God and Lord,
> With all your graces now outpoured

CONCLUSION

On each believer's mind and heart;
Your fervent love to them impart.
Lord, by the brightness of your light
In holy faith your Church unite;
From every land and every tongue
This to your praise, O Lord, our God, be sung:
Alleluia, Alleluia!

Come, holy Fire, comfort true,
Grant us the will your work to do
And in your service to abide;
Let trials turn us not aside.
Lord, by your power prepare each heart,
And to our weakness strength impart
That bravely here we may contend,
Through life and death to you, our Lord, ascend.
Alleluia, Alleluia!

> Martin Luther, 1524
> (taken from *Lutheran Worship,* © CPH 1982)

NOTES

PART 1 INTRODUCTION

1. Dean M. Kelly, *Why Conservative Churches Are Growing: A Study in Sociology of Religion* New York: Harper and Row, 1972).

PART 2 INTRODUCTION

1. W. Charles Arn, "Evangelism and Disciple Making," Institute of American Church Growth, Pasadena, Calif.
2. Flavil R. Yeakley, "Views of Evangelism," *The Pastor's Church Growth Handbook*, Vol. II, ed. by Win Arn (Pasadena: Church Growth Press, 1982).
3. Win Arn, Carroll Nyquist, Charles Arn, *Who Cares About Love?* (Pasadena: Church Growth Press, 1986).

CHAPTER 4

1. George Marsden, *Evangelicalism and Modern America* (Grand Rapids: Eerdmans, 1984), pp. ix–xv.
2. Ibid., p. ix.

CHAPTER 5

1. George Marsden, *Evangelicalism and Modern America* (Grand Rapids: Eerdmans, 1984), p. ix.
2. Carl Dudley, *Where Have All Our People Gone?* (New York: Pilgrim Press, 1979).
3. Dean R. Hoge and David A. Roozen, eds., *Understanding Church Growth and Decline: 1950–78* (New York: Pilgrim Press, 1979).
4. William Hordern, *Experience and Faith: The Significance of Luther for Understanding Today's Experiential Religion* (Minneapolis: Augsburg, 1983), pp. 98–99.

CHAPTER 6

1. Frederick E. Mayer, *The Religious Bodies of America,* 4th ed. rev. A. C. Piepkorn (St. Louis: Concordia, 1961).
2. Arthur Carl Piepkorn, *Profiles in Belief* (New York: Harper and Row, 1977, '78, '79).

NOTES

CHAPTER 7

1. Samuel S. Hill Jr., "The Shape and Shapes of Popular Southern Piety," *Varieties of Southern Evangelicalism* (Macon, Ga.: Mercer University Press, 1981), pp. 89–114.

2. Walter Bauer, William Arndt, F. Wilbur Gingrich, *A Greek-English Lexicon of the New Testament and Other Early Christian Literature,* rev. Frederick W. Danker (Chicago: University of Chicago Press, 1979), p. 661.

3. Hill, p. 100.

4. Interview with participants in Evangelism Conference of The Lutheran Church—Missouri Synod, May 16, 1986.

5. Hill, p. 102.

6. George Marsden, *Fundamentalism and American Culture: The Shaping of Twentieth-Century Evangelicalism: 1870–1925* (New York: Oxford University Press, 1980).

7. Hill, p. 100.

8. *Yearbook of American and Canadian Churches, 1987* (Nashville: Abingdon Press, 1987), pp. 254–55.

9. Hill, p. 109.

10. Norman Vincent Peale, *The True Joy of Positive Living: An Autobiography* (New York: Fawcett Press, 1984).

11. Professor Roberta Hestenes, former associate professor of Christian formation and discipleship, Fuller Theological Seminary, and chairperson of World Vision International, and now president of Eastern Baptist College, Philadelphia.

CHAPTER 8

1. Milton L. Rudnick, *Fundamentalism and the Missouri Synod: A Historical Study of Their Interaction and Mutual Influence* (St. Louis: Concordia, 1966).

2. The Large Catechism, *The Book of Concord,* trans. and ed. Theodore G. Tappert (Philadelphia: Fortress Press, 1959), p. 448. The specific form of this quote is from The Smalcald Articles, Tappert, p. 310.

3. John L. Peters, *Christian Perfection and American Methodism* (Francis Asbury Press, 1956, 1985), pp. 23–24. Dale Brown, *Understanding Pietism* (Grand Rapids: Eerdmans, 1978), p. 159.

4. See, for instance, Henry C. Dequin, "Pietism and the Traditional Worship Practices of the Lutheran Church," STM Thesis, Concordia Seminary, St. Louis, 1955.

5. Martin Marty, *A Short History of Christianity* (Cleveland: World Press, 1959), p. 275.

6. Stoeffler and Bloesch are cited in Brown.

7. Theodore G. Tappert, "The Influence of Pietism in Colonial Lutheranism," in *Continental Pietism and Early American Christianity,* ed. F. Ernest Stoeffler (Eerdmans, 1976), pp. 13–33.

8. Erich Hugo Heintzen, "Wilhelm Loehe and the Missouri Synod," Ph. D. dissertation, University of Illinois, 1964, p. 3.

9. Abdel Ross Wentz, *The Lutheran Church in American History* (Philadelphia: United Lutheran Publishing House, 1923), p. 151.
10. Interview in June 1986 and follow-up letter of Feb. 23, 1988, from James W. Albers, associate professor of theology and vice president for admissions, Valparaiso University.
11. C. F. W. Walther, *The Proper Distinction Between Law and Gospel,* trans. W. H. T. Dau (St. Louis: Concordia, 1929; 14th printing, 1986), pp. 196–97.

PART 3 INTRODUCTION

1. Nathan O. Hatch, "Evangelicalism as a Democratic Movement," *Evangelicalism and Modern America,* ed. George Marsden (Grand Rapids: Eerdmans, 1984), p. 72.

CHAPTER 9

1. Hatch, p. 73.
2. Richard Ostley, "Evangelical Publishing and Broadcasting," *Evangelicalism and Modern America,* pp. 48–49.
3. Hatch, pp. 73–74.

CHAPTER 11

1. George Marsden, *Evangelicalism and Modern America* (Grand Rapids: Eerdmans, 1984), p. ix.
2. Luther P. Gerlach and Virginia Hine, *People, Power, Changes: Movements of Social Transformation* (Indianapolis: Bobbs-Merrill, 1970).
3. *Mission Handbook: North American Protestant Ministries Overseas,* 12th ed. (Monrovia, Calif. MARC, 1979).
4. Jerry White, *The Church and the Parachurch: An Uneasy Marriage* (Portland: Multnoma Press, 1983), pp. 27–32.

CHAPTER 12

1. James Pragman, *Traditions of Ministry* (St. Louis: Concordia, 1983).
2. *The Book of Concord,* trans. and ed. Theodore G. Tappert (Philadelphia: Fortress Press, 1959), p. 214.
3. Johann Gerhard, as quoted in Pragman, p. 62.
4. Pragman, pp. 15–16.
5. Martin Luther, as quoted in Francis Pieper, *Christian Dogmatics,* Vol. III, trans. Walter W. F. Albrecht et al. (St. Louis: Concordia, 1953), p. 442.
6. Philip Jacob Spener, *Pia Desidera,* in *Pietists Selected Writings,* ed. Peter C. Erb (Ramsey, N.J.: Paulist Press, 1983), p. 36.